UNFINISHED BUSINESS™

UNFINISHED BUSINESS™

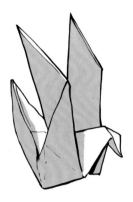

story
PAUL LEVITZ

art
SIMON FRASER

coloring
GARY CALDWELL and SIMON FRASER

lettering
NATE PIEKOS for BLAMBOT

dark horse books

president and publisher
MIKE RICHARDSON

editor
CHRIS WARNER

assistant editor
KONNER KNUDSEN

digital art technician
ADAM PRUETT

designer
PATRICK SATTERFIELD

UNFINISHED BUSINESS™

Unfinished Business is an original graphic novel, never before published.

Library of Congress Cataloging-in-Publication Data

Names: Levitz, Paul, author. | Fraser, Simon, 1969- artist. | Caldwell,
   Gary (Comic book artist), colourist. | Piekos, Nate, letterer.
Title: Unfinished business / story, Paul Levitz ; art, Simon Fraser ;
   coloring, Gary Caldwell and Simon Fraser ; lettering, Nate Piekos for
   Blambot.
Description: First edition. | Milwaukie, OR : Dark Horse Books, 2020. |
   Summary: "A priest, a minister and a rabbi walk into a bar . . . a
   would-be lead-in to an amusing anecdote were it not for the three being
   dead. But this is no zombie apocalypse (sorry, Walking Dead fans). The
   clerics have a bit of Unfinished Business tied to their demise that
   heaven needs them to address, if they can. But what is the reward for
   unraveling the riddle of their deaths–is it life, afterlife, or
   oblivion? Maybe they can ask the smiling bartender, who just might be
   God"-- Provided by publisher.
Identifiers: LCCN 2019060086 | ISBN 9781506720654 (hardcover)
Subjects: LCSH: Graphic novels.
Classification: LCC PN6727.L488 U54 2020 | DDC 741.5/973--dc23
LC record available at https://lccn.loc.gov/2019060086

DARK HORSE BOOKS
A division of Dark Horse Comics LLC
10956 SE Main Street
Milwaukie, OR 97222

DarkHorse.com

To find a comics shop in your area,
go to comicshoplocator.com

First edition: April 2021
ISBN 978-1-50672-065-4

10 9 8 7 6 5 4 3 2 1

Printed in China

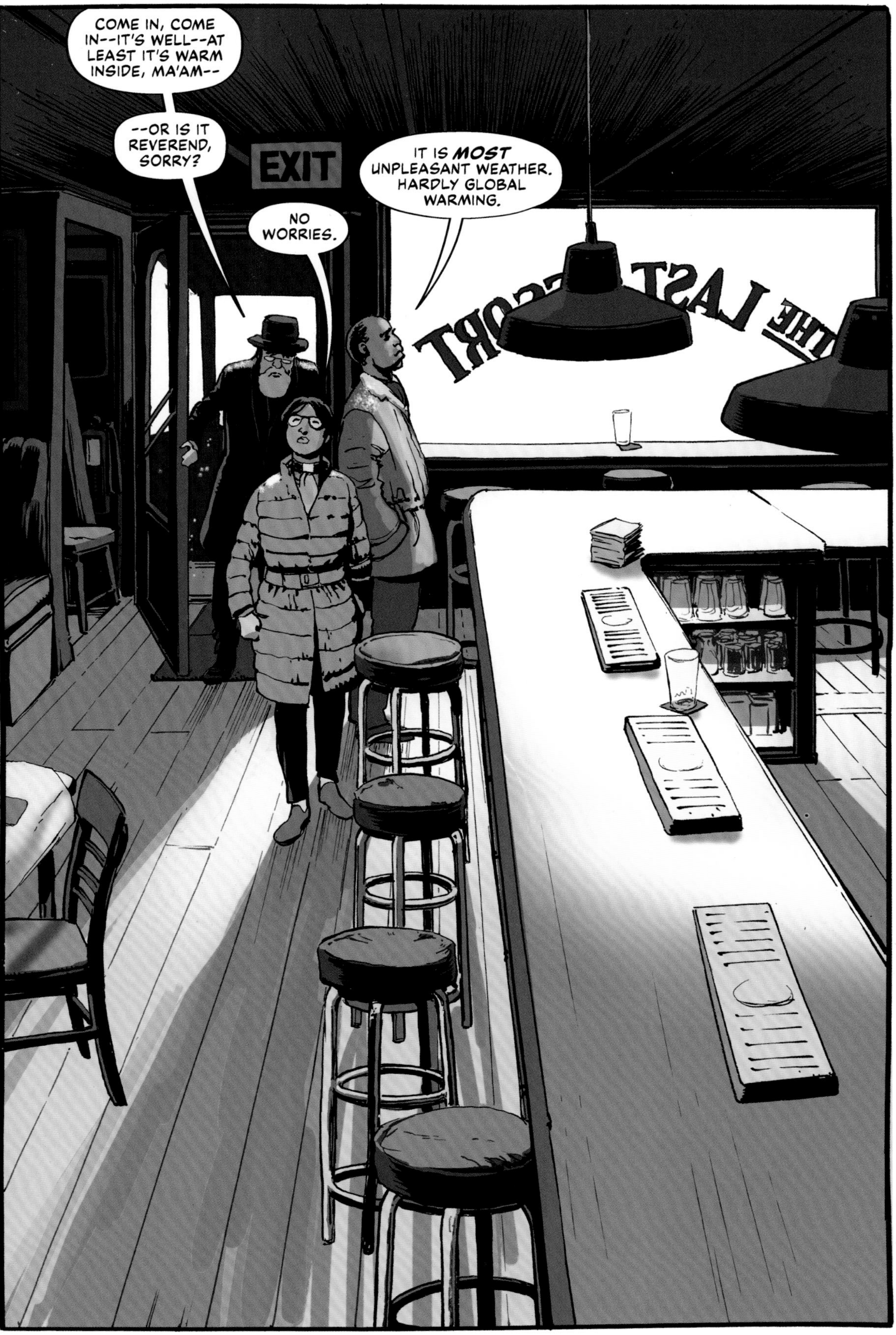
COME IN, COME IN--IT'S WELL--AT LEAST IT'S WARM INSIDE, MA'AM--
--OR IS IT REVEREND, SORRY?
EXIT
NO WORRIES.
IT IS *MOST* UNPLEASANT WEATHER. HARDLY GLOBAL WARMING.

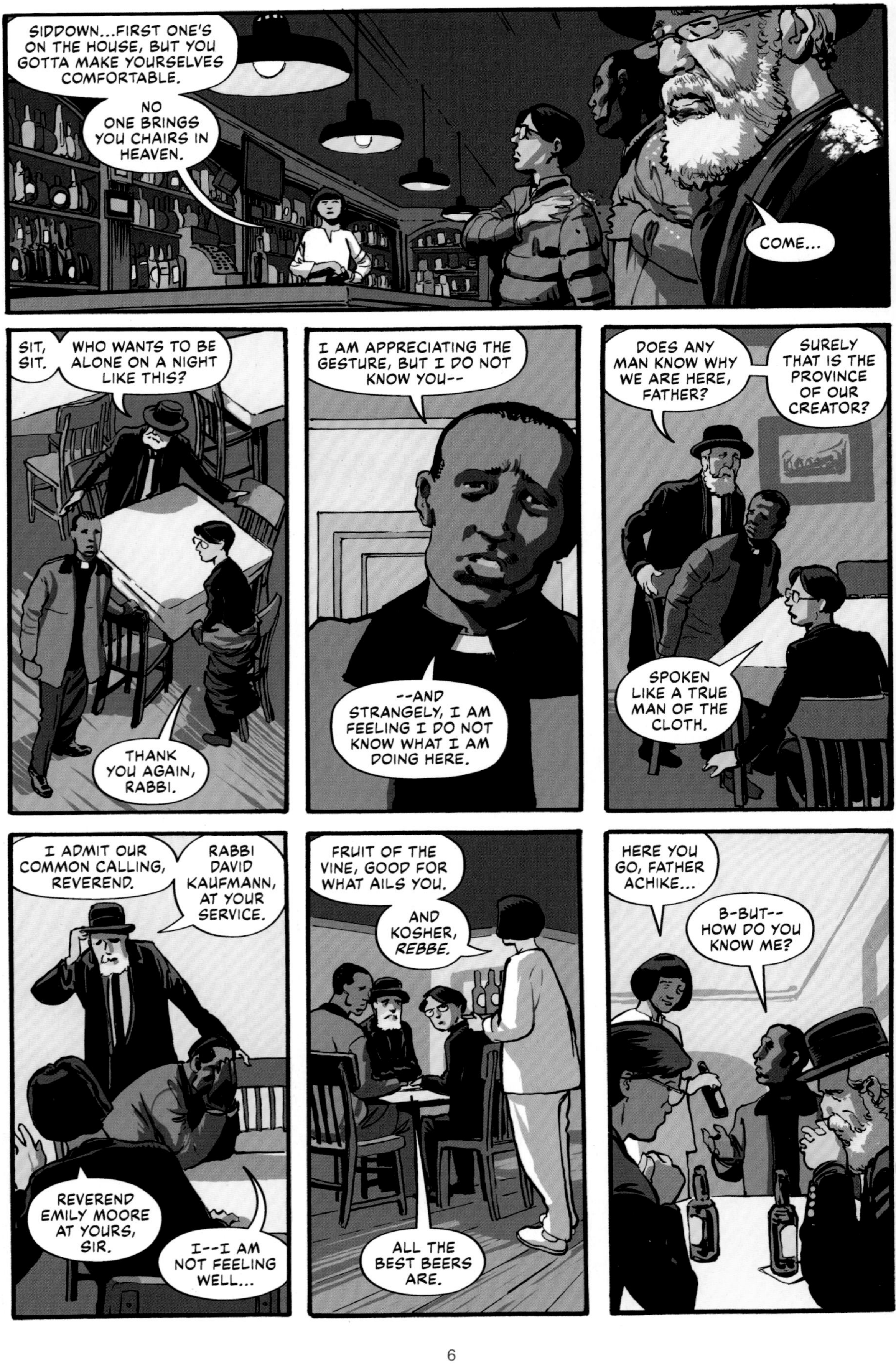
SIDDOWN...FIRST ONE'S ON THE HOUSE, BUT YOU GOTTA MAKE YOURSELVES COMFORTABLE.
NO ONE BRINGS YOU CHAIRS IN HEAVEN.
COME...
SIT, SIT.
WHO WANTS TO BE ALONE ON A NIGHT LIKE THIS?
THANK YOU AGAIN, RABBI.
I AM APPRECIATING THE GESTURE, BUT I DO NOT KNOW YOU--
--AND STRANGELY, I AM FEELING I DO NOT KNOW WHAT I AM DOING HERE.
DOES ANY MAN KNOW WHY WE ARE HERE, FATHER?
SURELY THAT IS THE PROVINCE OF OUR CREATOR?
SPOKEN LIKE A TRUE MAN OF THE CLOTH.
I ADMIT OUR COMMON CALLING, REVEREND.
RABBI DAVID KAUFMANN, AT YOUR SERVICE.
REVEREND EMILY MOORE AT YOURS, SIR.
I--I AM NOT FEELING WELL...
FRUIT OF THE VINE, GOOD FOR WHAT AILS YOU.
AND KOSHER, *REBBE.*
ALL THE BEST BEERS ARE.
HERE YOU GO, FATHER ACHIKE...
B-BUT-- HOW DO YOU KNOW ME?

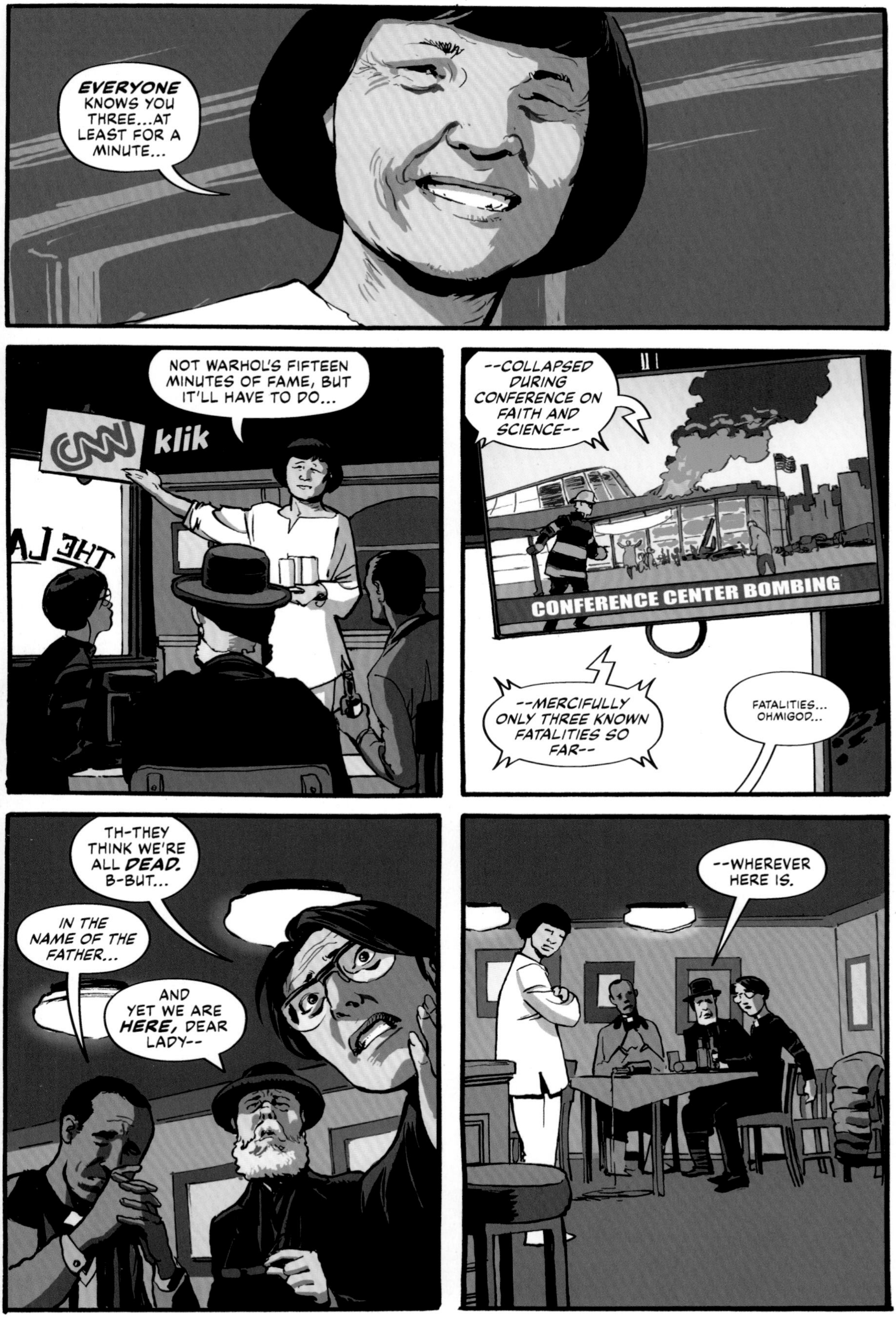
EVERYONE KNOWS YOU THREE...AT LEAST FOR A MINUTE...
NOT WARHOL'S FIFTEEN MINUTES OF FAME, BUT IT'LL HAVE TO DO...
CNN klik
--COLLAPSED DURING CONFERENCE ON FAITH AND SCIENCE--
CONFERENCE CENTER BOMBING
--MERCIFULLY ONLY THREE KNOWN FATALITIES SO FAR--
FATALITIES... OHMIGOD...
TH-THEY THINK WE'RE ALL DEAD. B-BUT...
IN THE NAME OF THE FATHER...
AND YET WE ARE HERE, DEAR LADY--
--WHEREVER HERE IS.

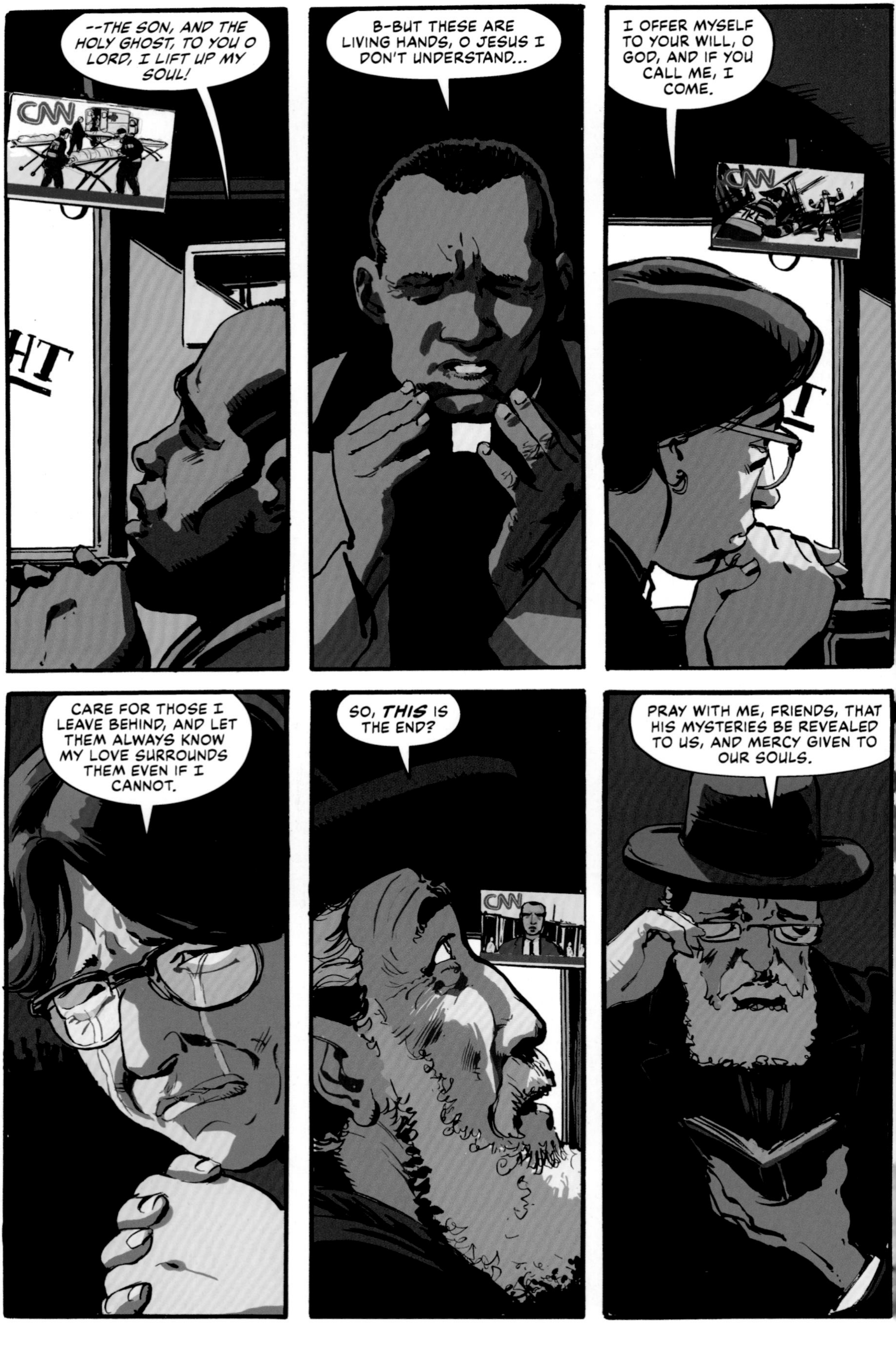
--THE SON, AND THE HOLY GHOST, TO YOU O LORD, I LIFT UP MY SOUL!
CNN
B-BUT THESE ARE LIVING HANDS, O JESUS I DON'T UNDERSTAND...
I OFFER MYSELF TO YOUR WILL, O GOD, AND IF YOU CALL ME, I COME.
CNN
CARE FOR THOSE I LEAVE BEHIND, AND LET THEM ALWAYS KNOW MY LOVE SURROUNDS THEM EVEN IF I CANNOT.
SO, THIS IS THE END?
CNN
PRAY WITH ME, FRIENDS, THAT HIS MYSTERIES BE REVEALED TO US, AND MERCY GIVEN TO OUR SOULS.

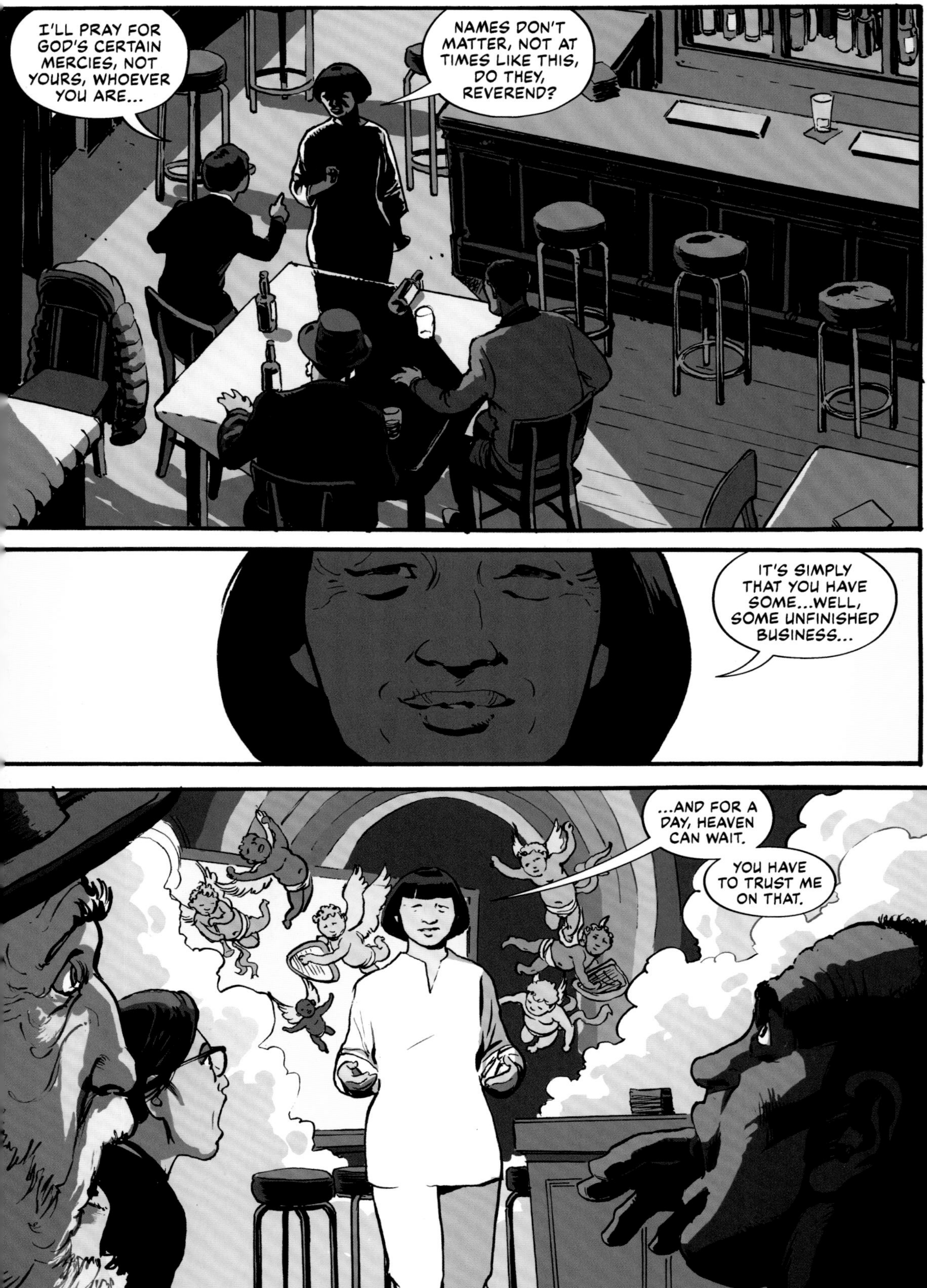
I'LL PRAY FOR GOD'S CERTAIN MERCIES, NOT YOURS, WHOEVER YOU ARE...
NAMES DON'T MATTER, NOT AT TIMES LIKE THIS, DO THEY, REVEREND?
IT'S SIMPLY THAT YOU HAVE SOME...WELL, SOME UNFINISHED BUSINESS...
...AND FOR A DAY, HEAVEN CAN WAIT.
YOU HAVE TO TRUST ME ON THAT.

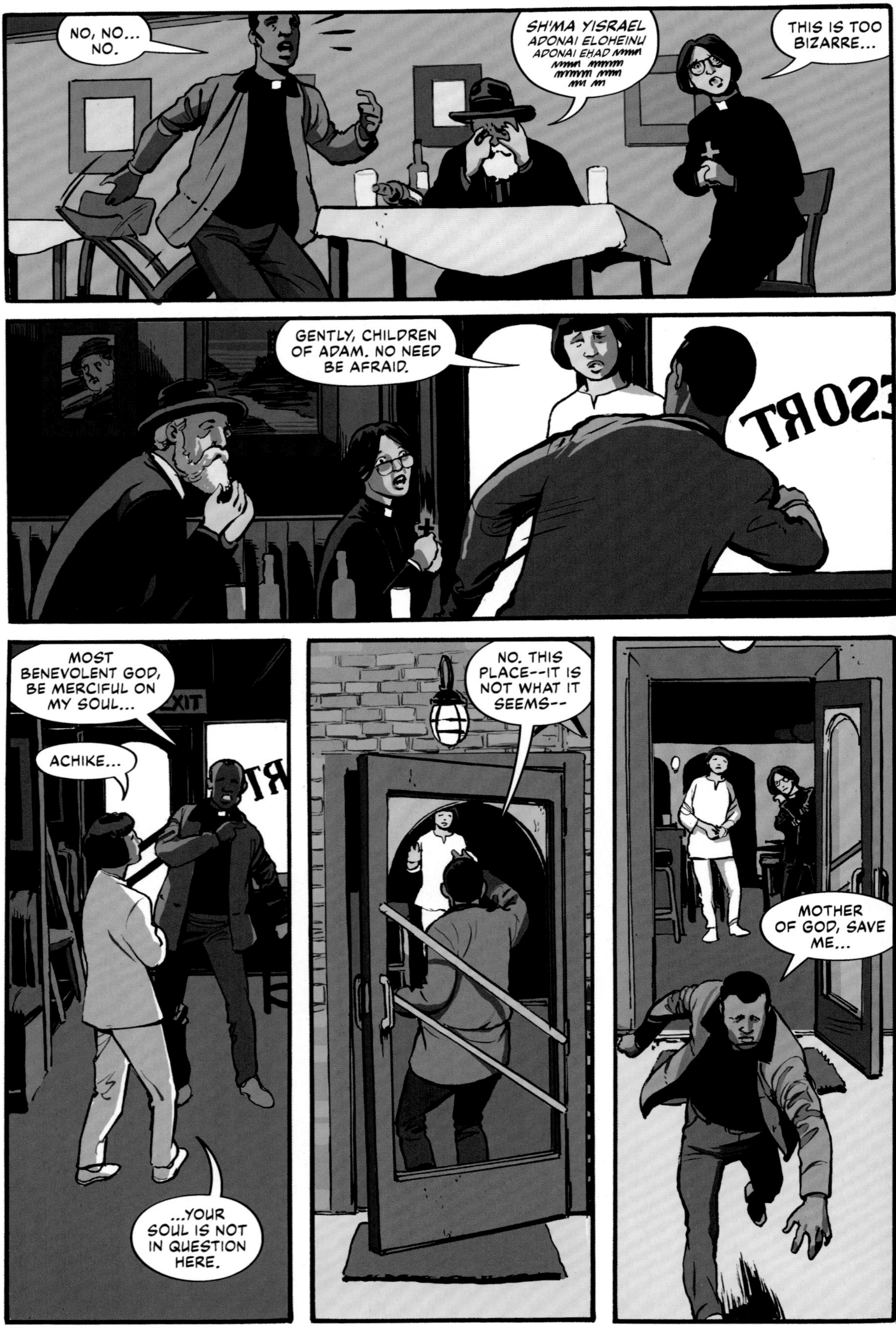

NO, NO... NO.
SH'MA YISRAEL ADONAI ELOHEINU ADONAI EHAD
THIS IS TOO BIZARRE...
GENTLY, CHILDREN OF ADAM. NO NEED BE AFRAID.
MOST BENEVOLENT GOD, BE MERCIFUL ON MY SOUL...
EXIT
ACHIKE...
...YOUR SOUL IS NOT IN QUESTION HERE.
NO. THIS PLACE--IT IS NOT WHAT IT SEEMS--
MOTHER OF GOD, SAVE ME...

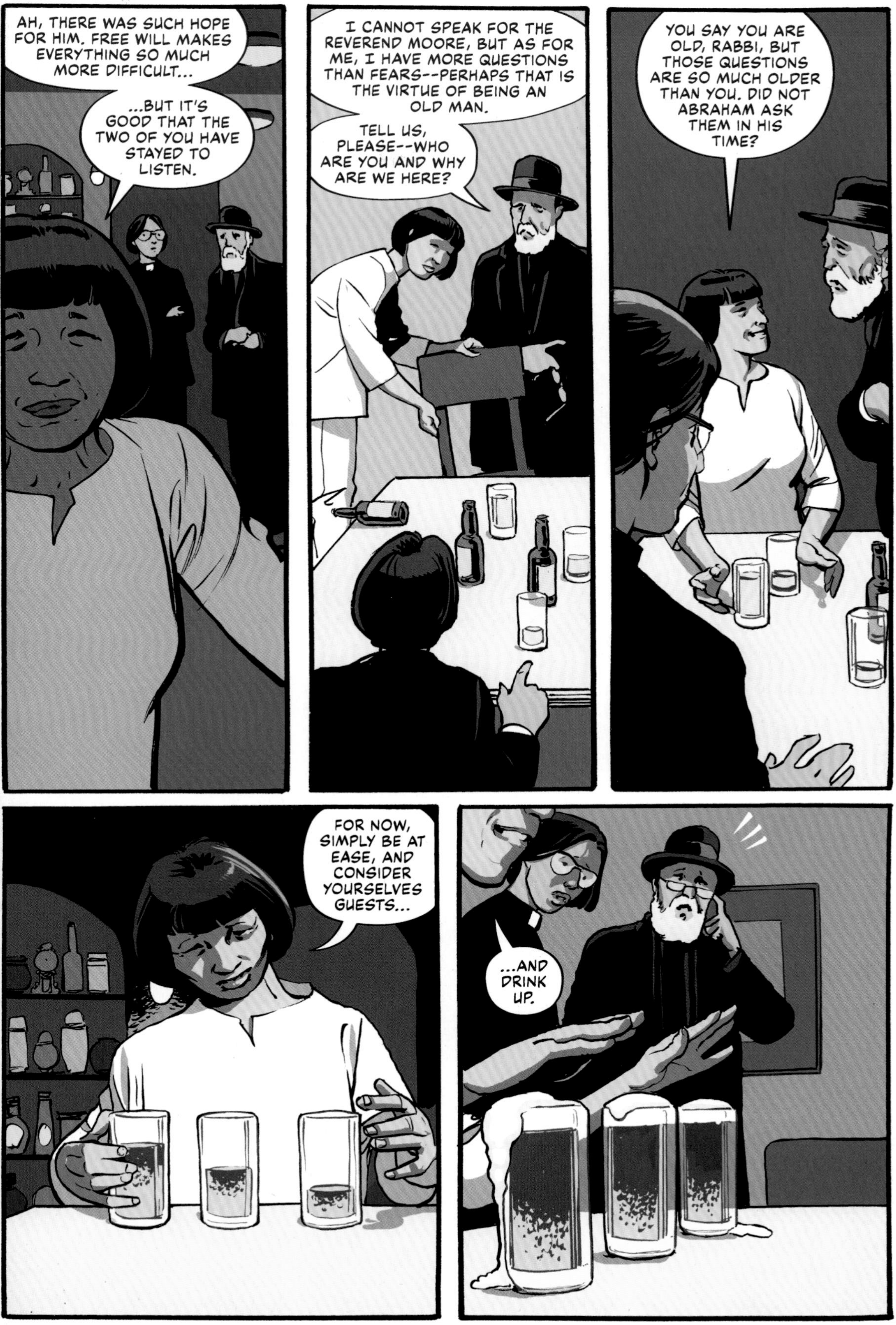
AH, THERE WAS SUCH HOPE FOR HIM. FREE WILL MAKES EVERYTHING SO MUCH MORE DIFFICULT...
...BUT IT'S GOOD THAT THE TWO OF YOU HAVE STAYED TO LISTEN.
I CANNOT SPEAK FOR THE REVEREND MOORE, BUT AS FOR ME, I HAVE MORE QUESTIONS THAN FEARS--PERHAPS THAT IS THE VIRTUE OF BEING AN OLD MAN.
TELL US, PLEASE--WHO ARE YOU AND WHY ARE WE HERE?
YOU SAY YOU ARE OLD, RABBI, BUT THOSE QUESTIONS ARE SO MUCH OLDER THAN YOU. DID NOT ABRAHAM ASK THEM IN HIS TIME?
FOR NOW, SIMPLY BE AT EASE, AND CONSIDER YOURSELVES GUESTS...
...AND DRINK UP.

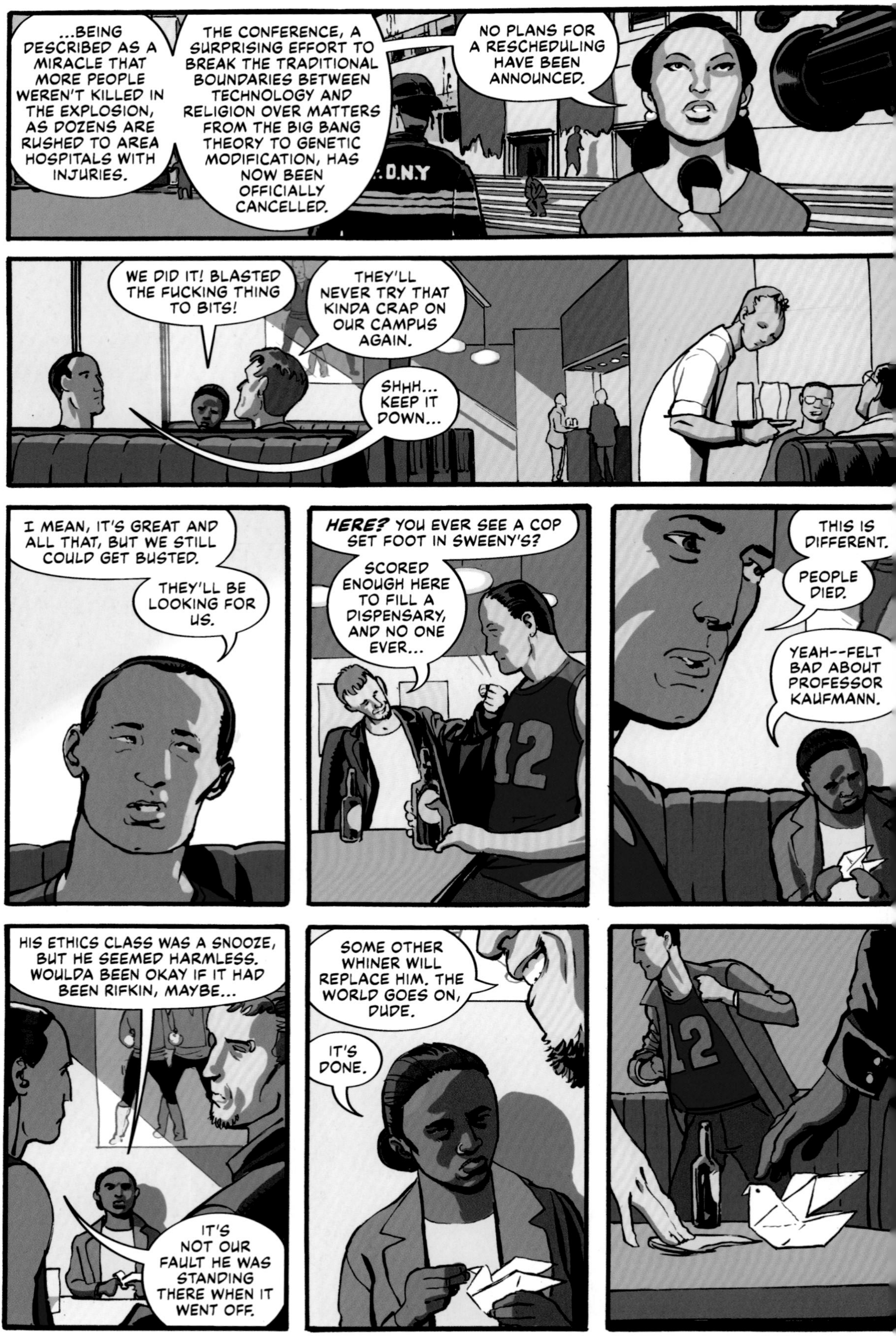
...BEING DESCRIBED AS A MIRACLE THAT MORE PEOPLE WEREN'T KILLED IN THE EXPLOSION, AS DOZENS ARE RUSHED TO AREA HOSPITALS WITH INJURIES.
THE CONFERENCE, A SURPRISING EFFORT TO BREAK THE TRADITIONAL BOUNDARIES BETWEEN TECHNOLOGY AND RELIGION OVER MATTERS FROM THE BIG BANG THEORY TO GENETIC MODIFICATION, HAS NOW BEEN OFFICIALLY CANCELLED.
NO PLANS FOR A RESCHEDULING HAVE BEEN ANNOUNCED.
WE DID IT! BLASTED THE FUCKING THING TO BITS!
THEY'LL NEVER TRY THAT KINDA CRAP ON OUR CAMPUS AGAIN.
SHHH... KEEP IT DOWN...
I MEAN, IT'S GREAT AND ALL THAT, BUT WE STILL COULD GET BUSTED.
THEY'LL BE LOOKING FOR US.
HERE? YOU EVER SEE A COP SET FOOT IN SWEENY'S?
SCORED ENOUGH HERE TO FILL A DISPENSARY, AND NO ONE EVER...
THIS IS DIFFERENT.
PEOPLE DIED.
YEAH--FELT BAD ABOUT PROFESSOR KAUFMANN.
HIS ETHICS CLASS WAS A SNOOZE, BUT HE SEEMED HARMLESS. WOULDA BEEN OKAY IF IT HAD BEEN RIFKIN, MAYBE...
IT'S NOT OUR FAULT HE WAS STANDING THERE WHEN IT WENT OFF.
SOME OTHER WHINER WILL REPLACE HIM. THE WORLD GOES ON, DUDE.
IT'S DONE.

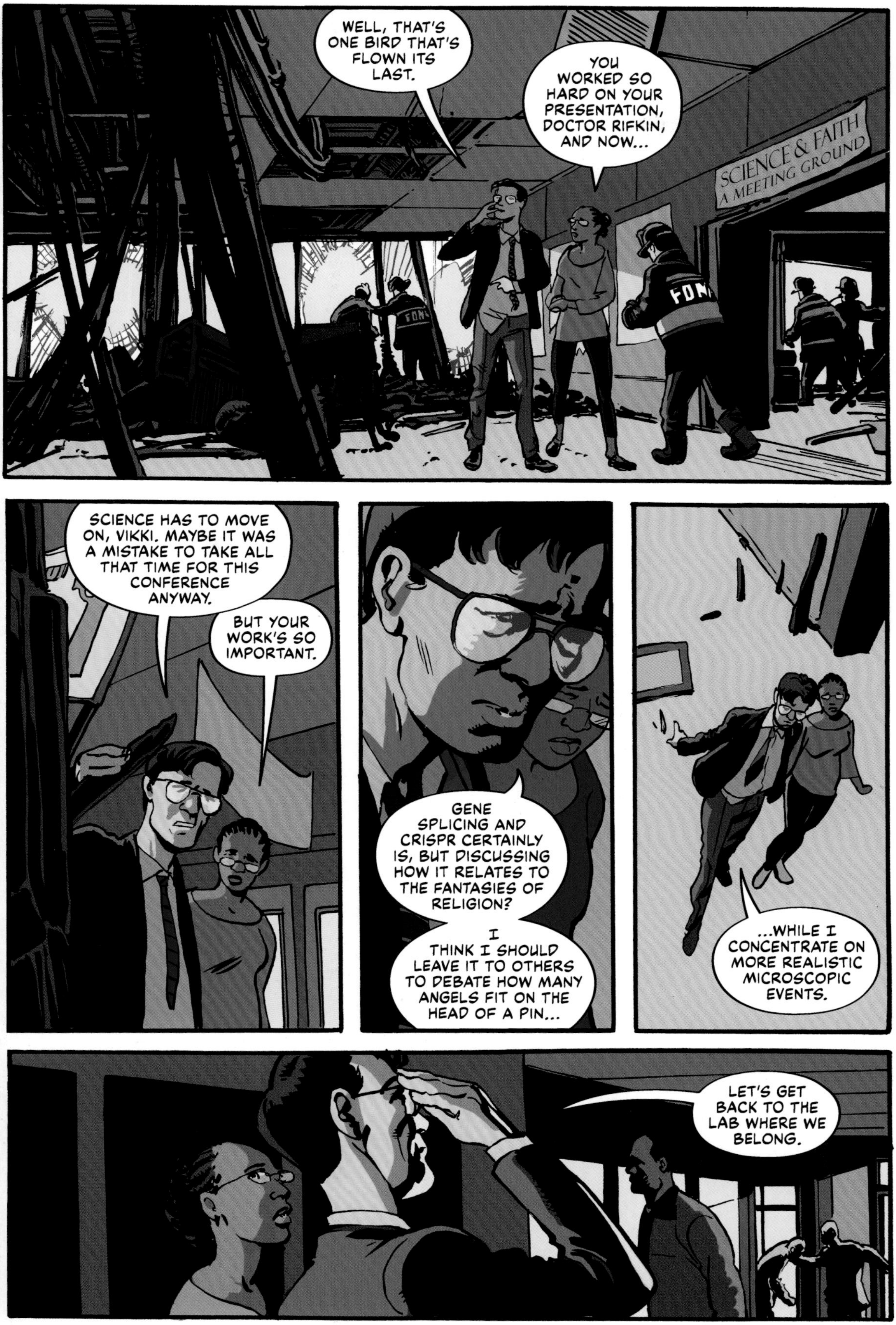
WELL, THAT'S ONE BIRD THAT'S FLOWN ITS LAST.
YOU WORKED SO HARD ON YOUR PRESENTATION, DOCTOR RIFKIN, AND NOW...
SCIENCE & FAITH
A MEETING GROUND
SCIENCE HAS TO MOVE ON, VIKKI. MAYBE IT WAS A MISTAKE TO TAKE ALL THAT TIME FOR THIS CONFERENCE ANYWAY.
BUT YOUR WORK'S SO IMPORTANT.
GENE SPLICING AND CRISPR CERTAINLY IS, BUT DISCUSSING HOW IT RELATES TO THE FANTASIES OF RELIGION?
I THINK I SHOULD LEAVE IT TO OTHERS TO DEBATE HOW MANY ANGELS FIT ON THE HEAD OF A PIN...
...WHILE I CONCENTRATE ON MORE REALISTIC MICROSCOPIC EVENTS.
LET'S GET BACK TO THE LAB WHERE WE BELONG.

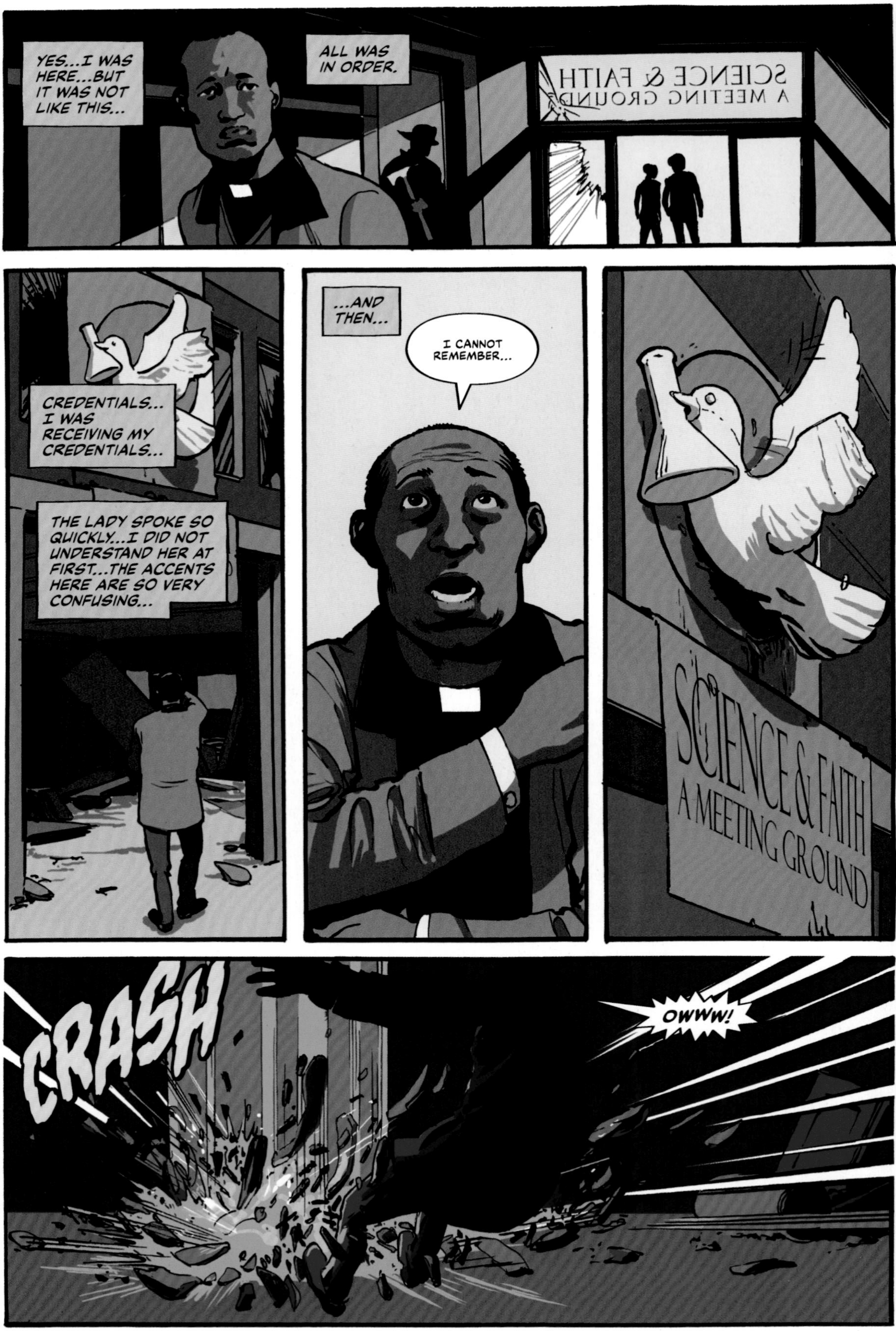
YES...I WAS HERE...BUT IT WAS NOT LIKE THIS...
ALL WAS IN ORDER.
SCIENCE & FAITH
A MEETING GROUND
CREDENTIALS... I WAS RECEIVING MY CREDENTIALS...
THE LADY SPOKE SO QUICKLY...I DID NOT UNDERSTAND HER AT FIRST...THE ACCENTS HERE ARE SO VERY CONFUSING...
...AND THEN...
I CANNOT REMEMBER...
SCIENCE & FAITH
A MEETING GROUND
CRASH
OWWW!

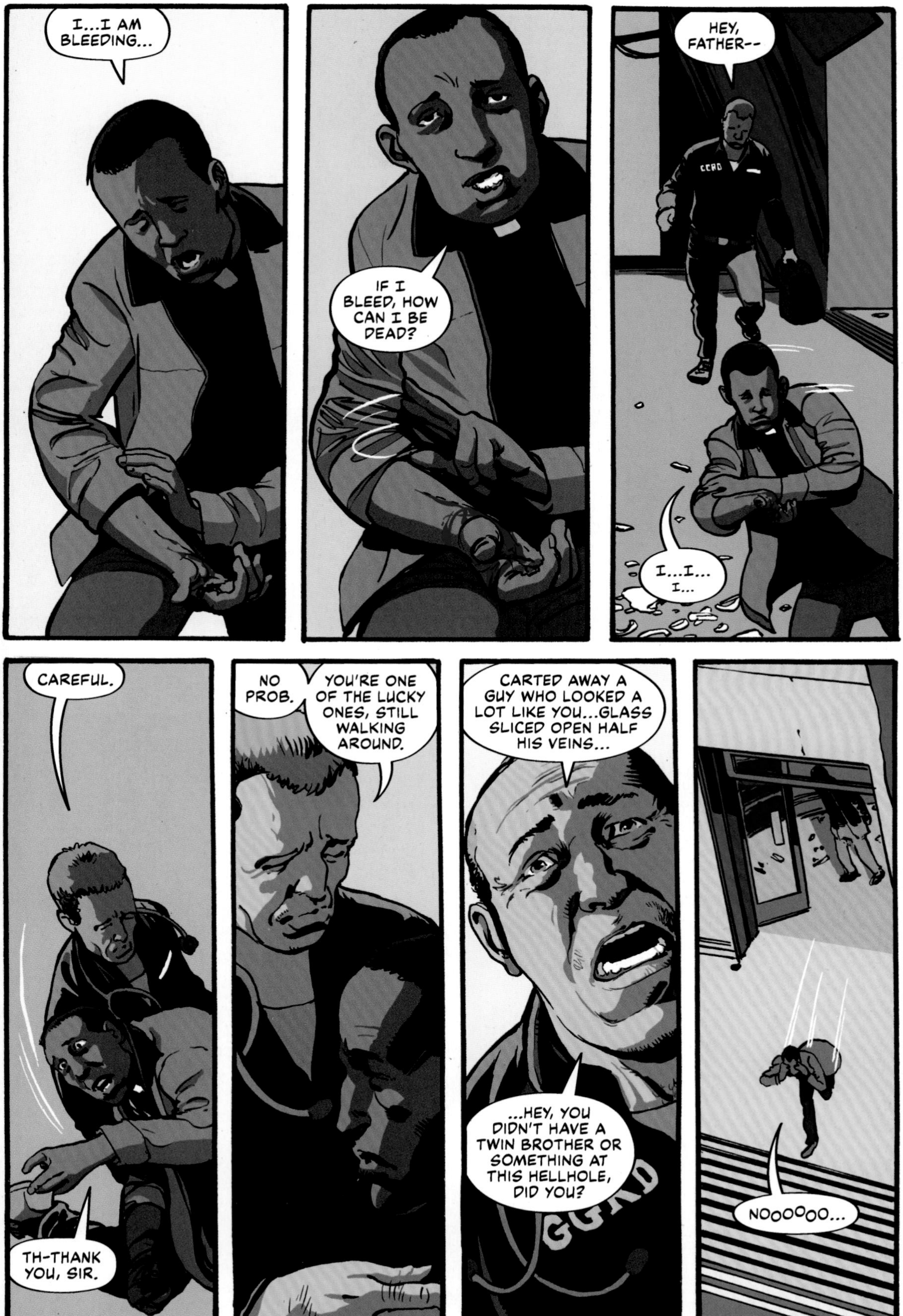
I...I AM BLEEDING...
IF I BLEED, HOW CAN I BE DEAD?
HEY, FATHER--
I...I... I...
CAREFUL.
TH-THANK YOU, SIR.
NO PROB.
YOU'RE ONE OF THE LUCKY ONES, STILL WALKING AROUND.
CARTED AWAY A GUY WHO LOOKED A LOT LIKE YOU...GLASS SLICED OPEN HALF HIS VEINS...
...HEY, YOU DIDN'T HAVE A TWIN BROTHER OR SOMETHING AT THIS HELLHOLE, DID YOU?
NOOOOOO...

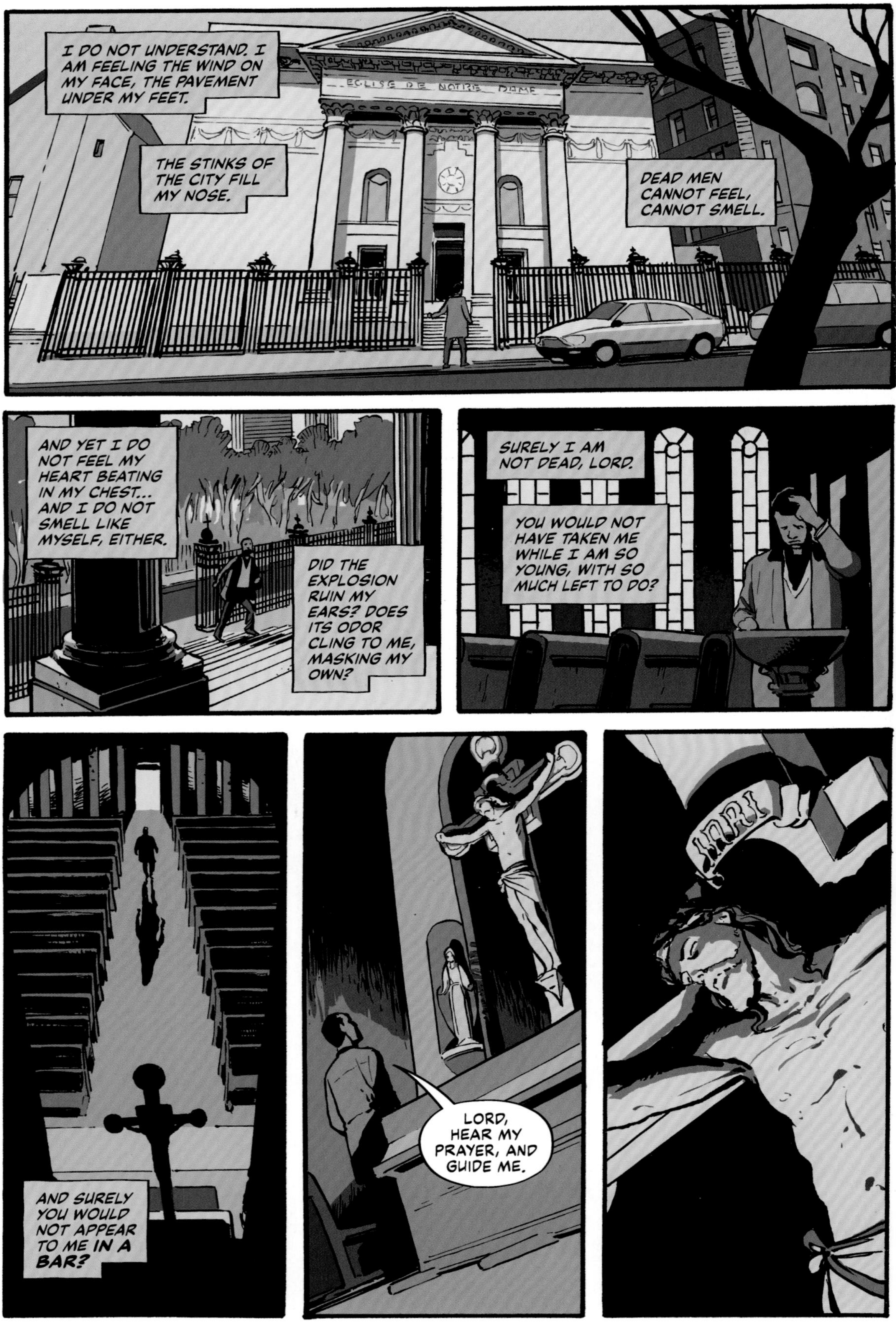
EGLISE DE NOTRE DAME
I DO NOT UNDERSTAND. I AM FEELING THE WIND ON MY FACE, THE PAVEMENT UNDER MY FEET.
THE STINKS OF THE CITY FILL MY NOSE.
DEAD MEN CANNOT FEEL, CANNOT SMELL.
AND YET I DO NOT FEEL MY HEART BEATING IN MY CHEST... AND I DO NOT SMELL LIKE MYSELF, EITHER.
DID THE EXPLOSION RUIN MY EARS? DOES ITS ODOR CLING TO ME, MASKING MY OWN?
SURELY I AM NOT DEAD, LORD.
YOU WOULD NOT HAVE TAKEN ME WHILE I AM SO YOUNG, WITH SO MUCH LEFT TO DO?
AND SURELY YOU WOULD NOT APPEAR TO ME IN A BAR?
LORD, HEAR MY PRAYER, AND GUIDE ME.
INRI

LORD, I HAVE STRUGGLED TO BE A GOOD MAN...

...TO LIVE MY LIFE AS YOU WOULD WISH.

THIS I HAVE DONE SINCE I WAS A SMALL BOY, AND HEARD THE WORDS MONSEIGNEUR BARRY SPOKE AT THE MISSION...

...THE WORDS THAT MADE YOU REAL IN MY MIND.

I FOUND MY CALLING, AND DID YOU HONOR WITH MY SACRIFICES...

...WITH ALL THE ACTS I PERFORMED SINCE I ACKNOWLEDGED YOU AS MY SAVIOR.

SAVE ME AGAIN NOW, LORD...

...AND GRANT ME THE STRENGTH TO CARRY ON.

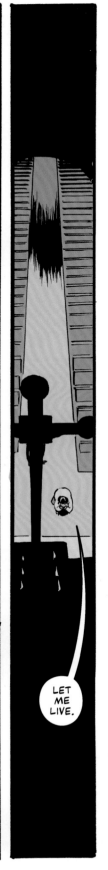

LET ME LIVE.

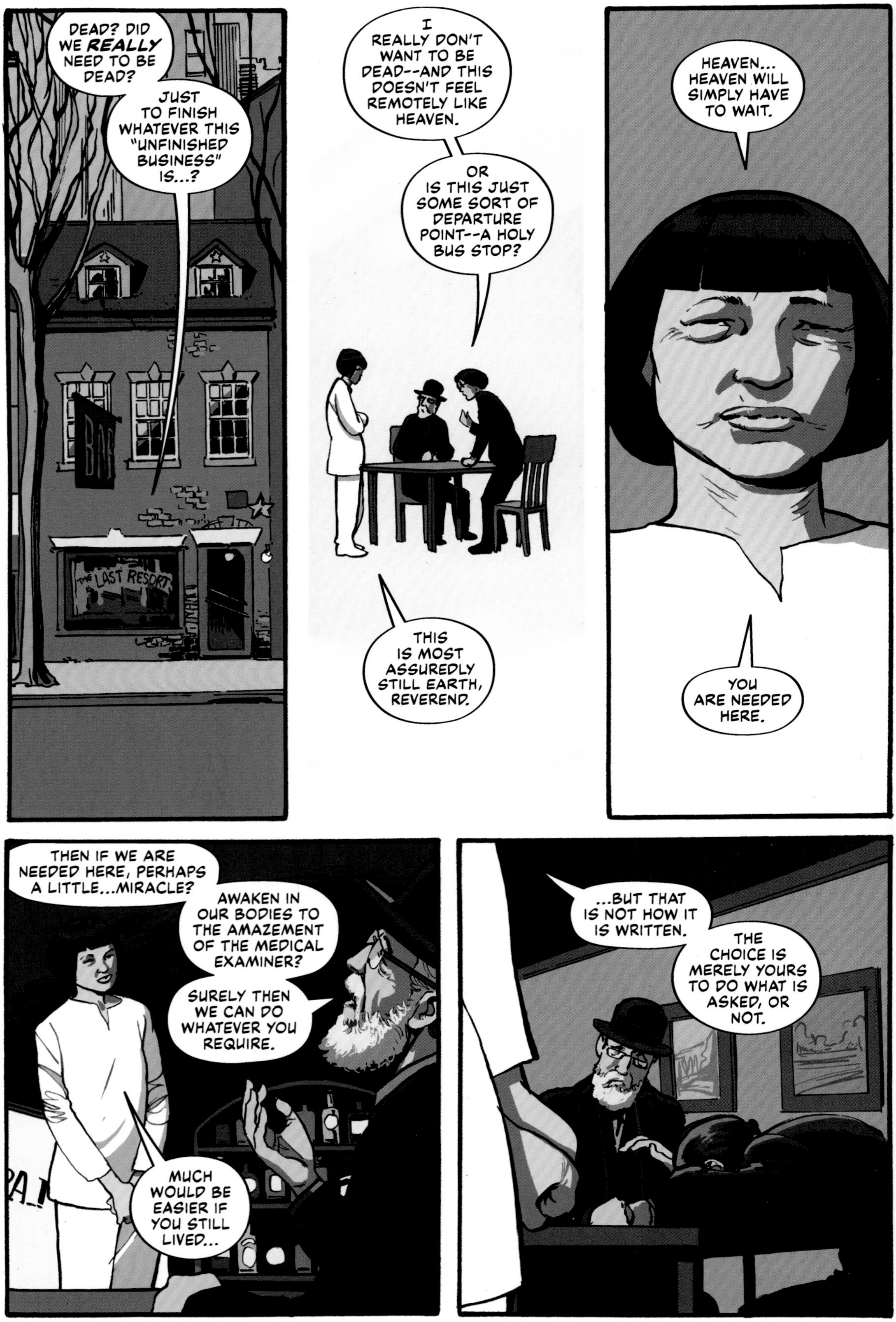
DEAD? DID WE *REALLY* NEED TO BE DEAD?
JUST TO FINISH WHATEVER THIS "UNFINISHED BUSINESS" IS...?
I REALLY DON'T WANT TO BE DEAD--AND THIS DOESN'T FEEL REMOTELY LIKE HEAVEN.
OR IS THIS JUST SOME SORT OF DEPARTURE POINT--A HOLY BUS STOP?
THIS IS MOST ASSUREDLY STILL EARTH, REVEREND.
HEAVEN... HEAVEN WILL SIMPLY HAVE TO WAIT.
YOU ARE NEEDED HERE.
THEN IF WE ARE NEEDED HERE, PERHAPS A LITTLE...MIRACLE?
AWAKEN IN OUR BODIES TO THE AMAZEMENT OF THE MEDICAL EXAMINER?
SURELY THEN WE CAN DO WHATEVER YOU REQUIRE.
MUCH WOULD BE EASIER IF YOU STILL LIVED...
...BUT THAT IS NOT HOW IT IS WRITTEN.
THE CHOICE IS MERELY YOURS TO DO WHAT IS ASKED, OR NOT.

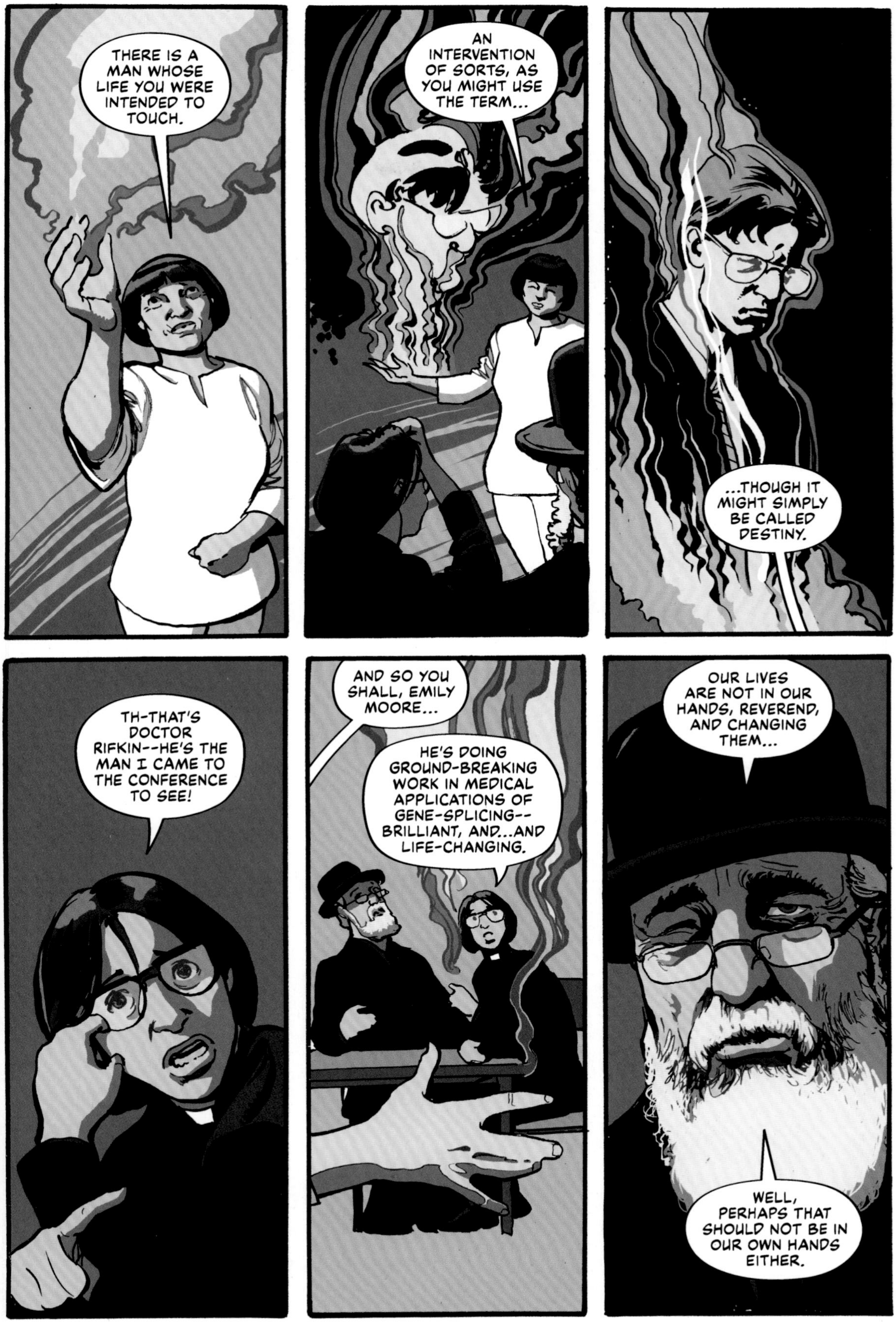
THERE IS A MAN WHOSE LIFE YOU WERE INTENDED TO TOUCH.
AN INTERVENTION OF SORTS, AS YOU MIGHT USE THE TERM...
...THOUGH IT MIGHT SIMPLY BE CALLED DESTINY.
TH-THAT'S DOCTOR RIFKIN--HE'S THE MAN I CAME TO THE CONFERENCE TO SEE!
AND SO YOU SHALL, EMILY MOORE...
HE'S DOING GROUND-BREAKING WORK IN MEDICAL APPLICATIONS OF GENE-SPLICING--BRILLIANT, AND...AND LIFE-CHANGING.
OUR LIVES ARE NOT IN OUR HANDS, REVEREND, AND CHANGING THEM...
WELL, PERHAPS THAT SHOULD NOT BE IN OUR OWN HANDS EITHER.

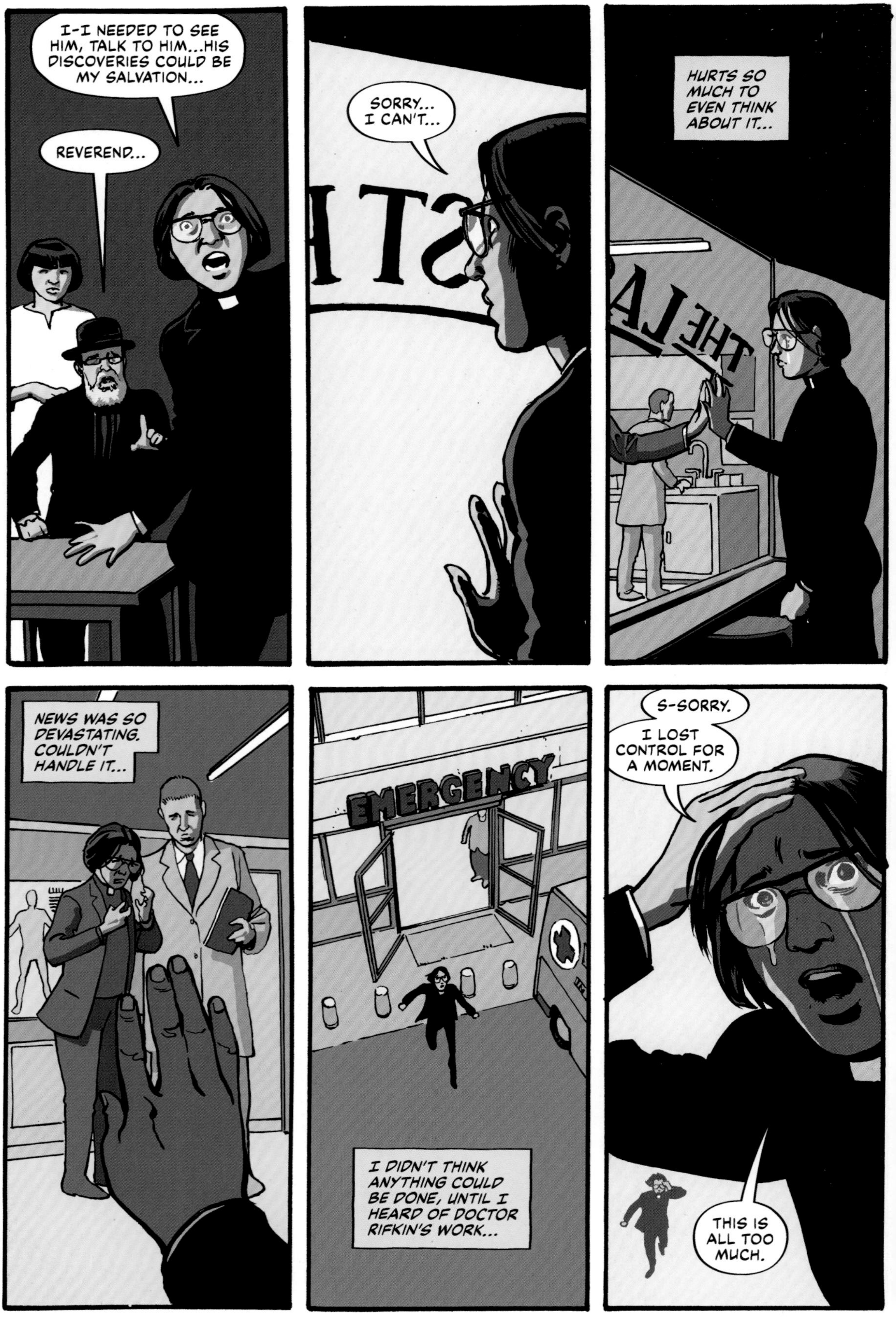
I-I NEEDED TO SEE HIM, TALK TO HIM...HIS DISCOVERIES COULD BE MY SALVATION...
REVEREND...
SORRY... I CAN'T...
HURTS SO MUCH TO EVEN THINK ABOUT IT...
NEWS WAS SO DEVASTATING. COULDN'T HANDLE IT...
EMERGENCY
I DIDN'T THINK ANYTHING COULD BE DONE, UNTIL I HEARD OF DOCTOR RIFKIN'S WORK...
S-SORRY.
I LOST CONTROL FOR A MOMENT.
THIS IS ALL TOO MUCH.

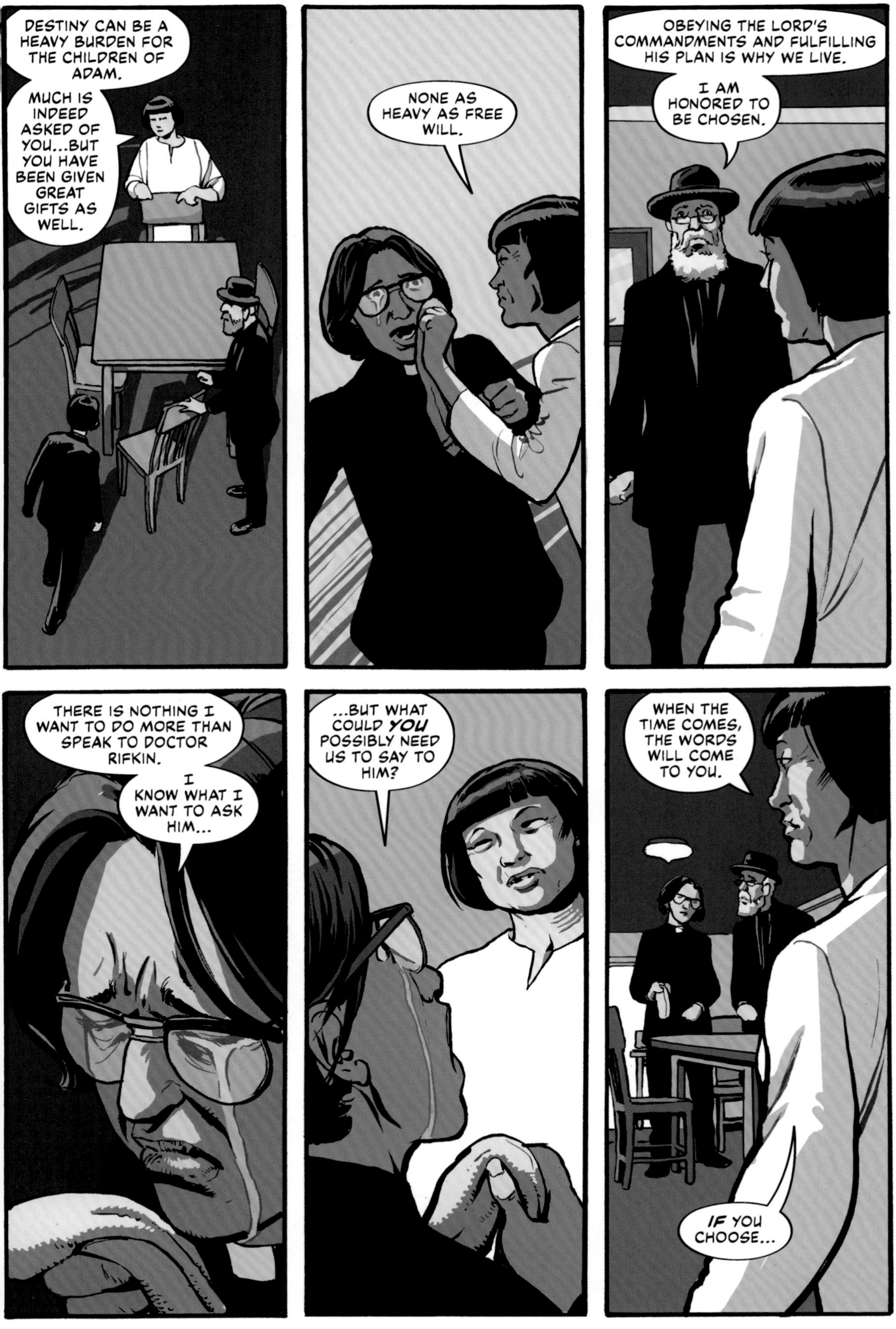
DESTINY CAN BE A HEAVY BURDEN FOR THE CHILDREN OF ADAM.
MUCH IS INDEED ASKED OF YOU...BUT YOU HAVE BEEN GIVEN GREAT GIFTS AS WELL.
NONE AS HEAVY AS FREE WILL.
OBEYING THE LORD'S COMMANDMENTS AND FULFILLING HIS PLAN IS WHY WE LIVE.
I AM HONORED TO BE CHOSEN.
THERE IS NOTHING I WANT TO DO MORE THAN SPEAK TO DOCTOR RIFKIN.
I KNOW WHAT I WANT TO ASK HIM...
...BUT WHAT COULD *YOU* POSSIBLY NEED US TO SAY TO HIM?
WHEN THE TIME COMES, THE WORDS WILL COME TO YOU.
IF YOU CHOOSE...

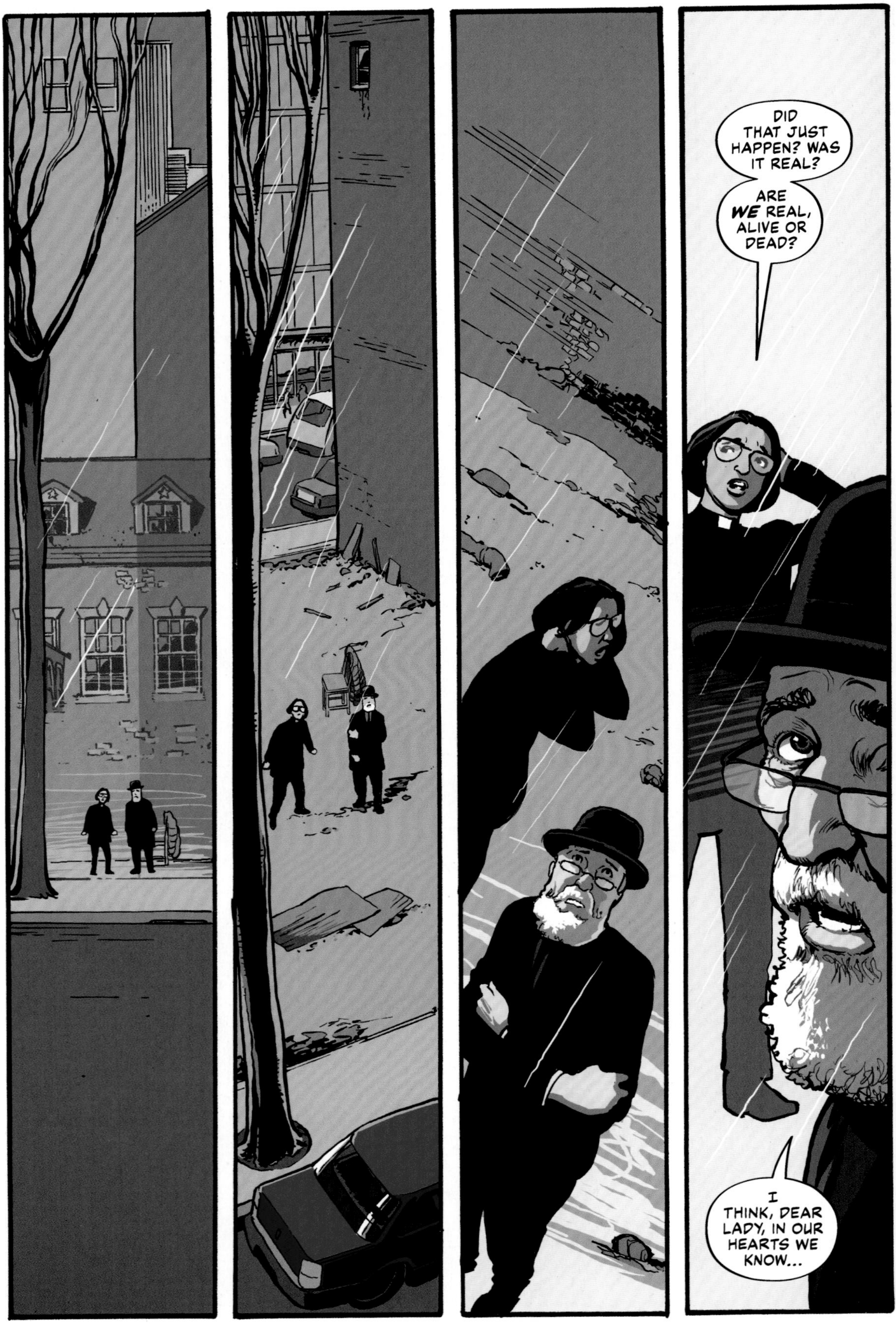
DID THAT JUST HAPPEN? WAS IT REAL?
ARE *WE* REAL, ALIVE OR DEAD?
I THINK, DEAR LADY, IN OUR HEARTS WE KNOW...

SO IF KAUFMANN'S TOAST, DO I STILL GET CREDIT FOR HIS COURSE?

OR DO I HAVE TO START SOME OTHER NONSENSE TO FULFILL THAT REQUIREMENT?

PAST THE DROP/ADD DATE...BET THEY'LL GET SOMEONE ELSE TO COVER THE CLASS.

ALL YOU HAVE TO DO IS COZY UP TO ANOTHER OLD DUDE.

THAT'S NOT HOW I GET *MY* GRADES, BEN.

I WORK MY TAIL OFF.

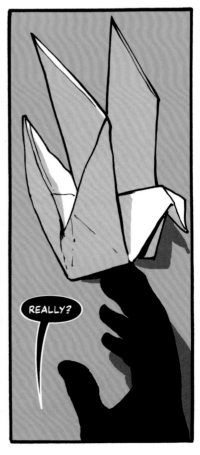

REALLY?

23

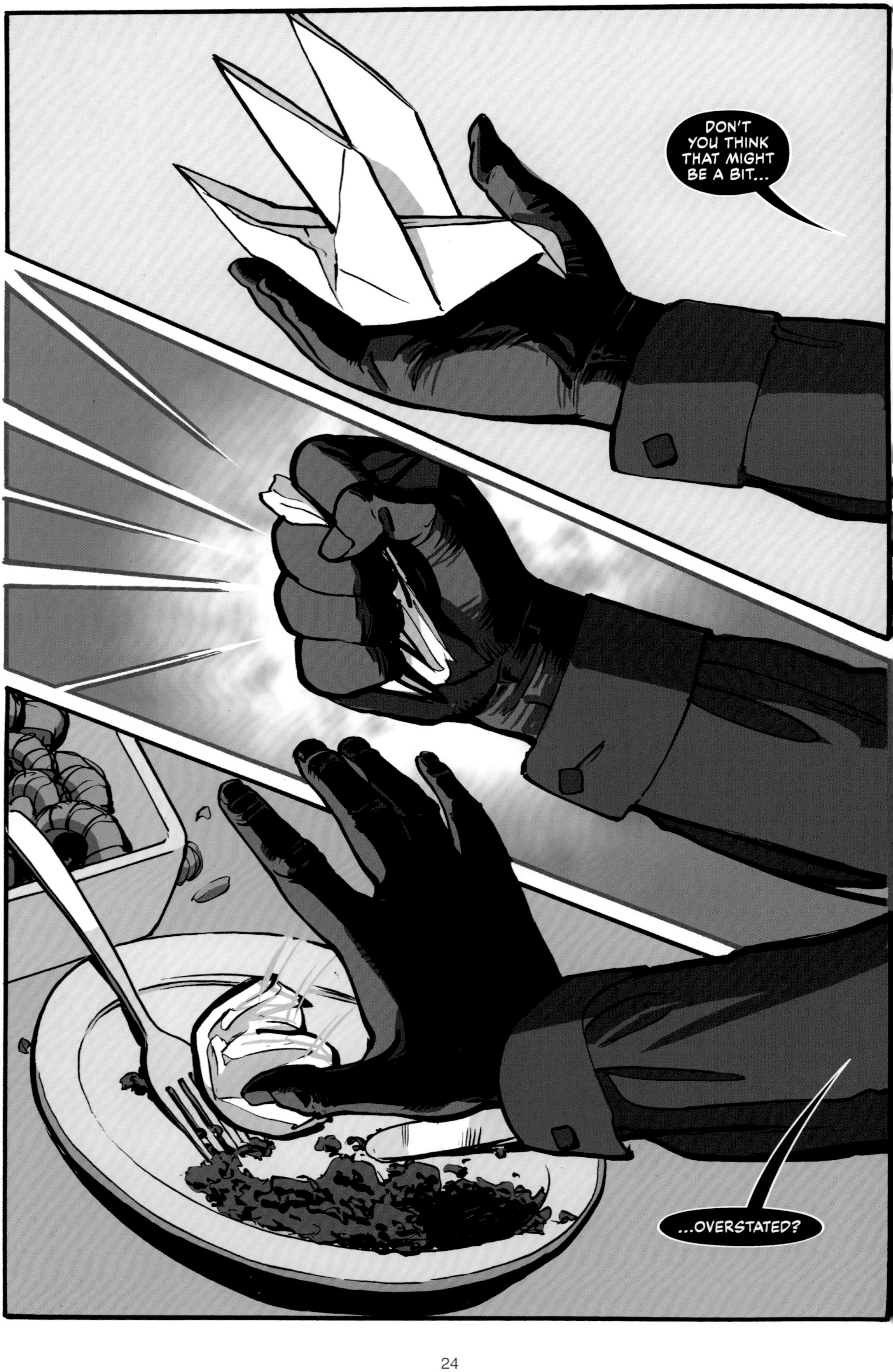
DON'T YOU THINK THAT MIGHT BE A BIT...
...OVERSTATED?

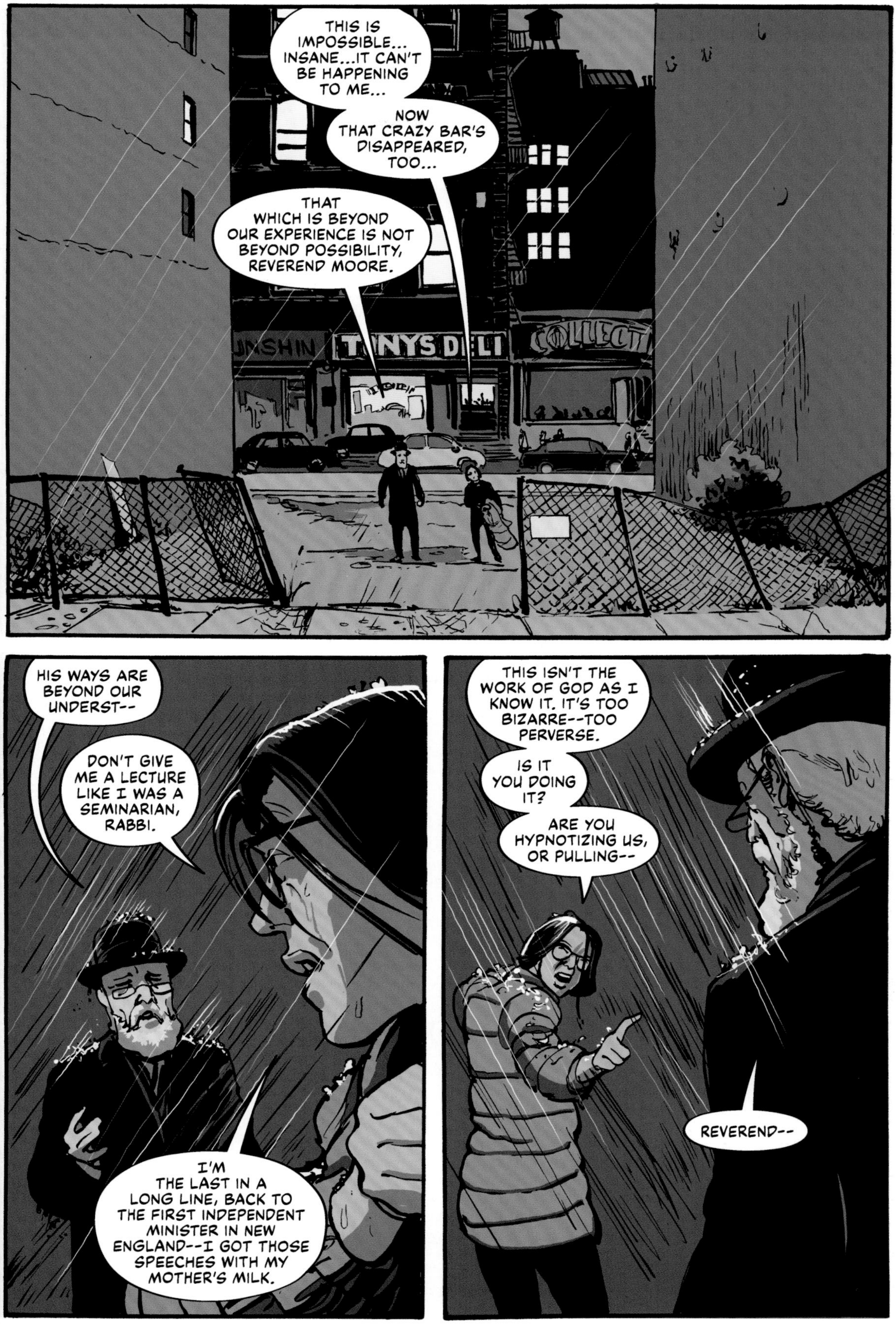
THIS IS IMPOSSIBLE... INSANE...IT CAN'T BE HAPPENING TO ME...
NOW THAT CRAZY BAR'S DISAPPEARED, TOO...
THAT WHICH IS BEYOND OUR EXPERIENCE IS NOT BEYOND POSSIBILITY, REVEREND MOORE.
TONYS DELI
HIS WAYS ARE BEYOND OUR UNDERST--
DON'T GIVE ME A LECTURE LIKE I WAS A SEMINARIAN, RABBI.
I'M THE LAST IN A LONG LINE, BACK TO THE FIRST INDEPENDENT MINISTER IN NEW ENGLAND--I GOT THOSE SPEECHES WITH MY MOTHER'S MILK.
THIS ISN'T THE WORK OF GOD AS I KNOW IT. IT'S TOO BIZARRE--TOO PERVERSE.
IS IT YOU DOING IT?
ARE YOU HYPNOTIZING US, OR PULLING--
REVEREND--

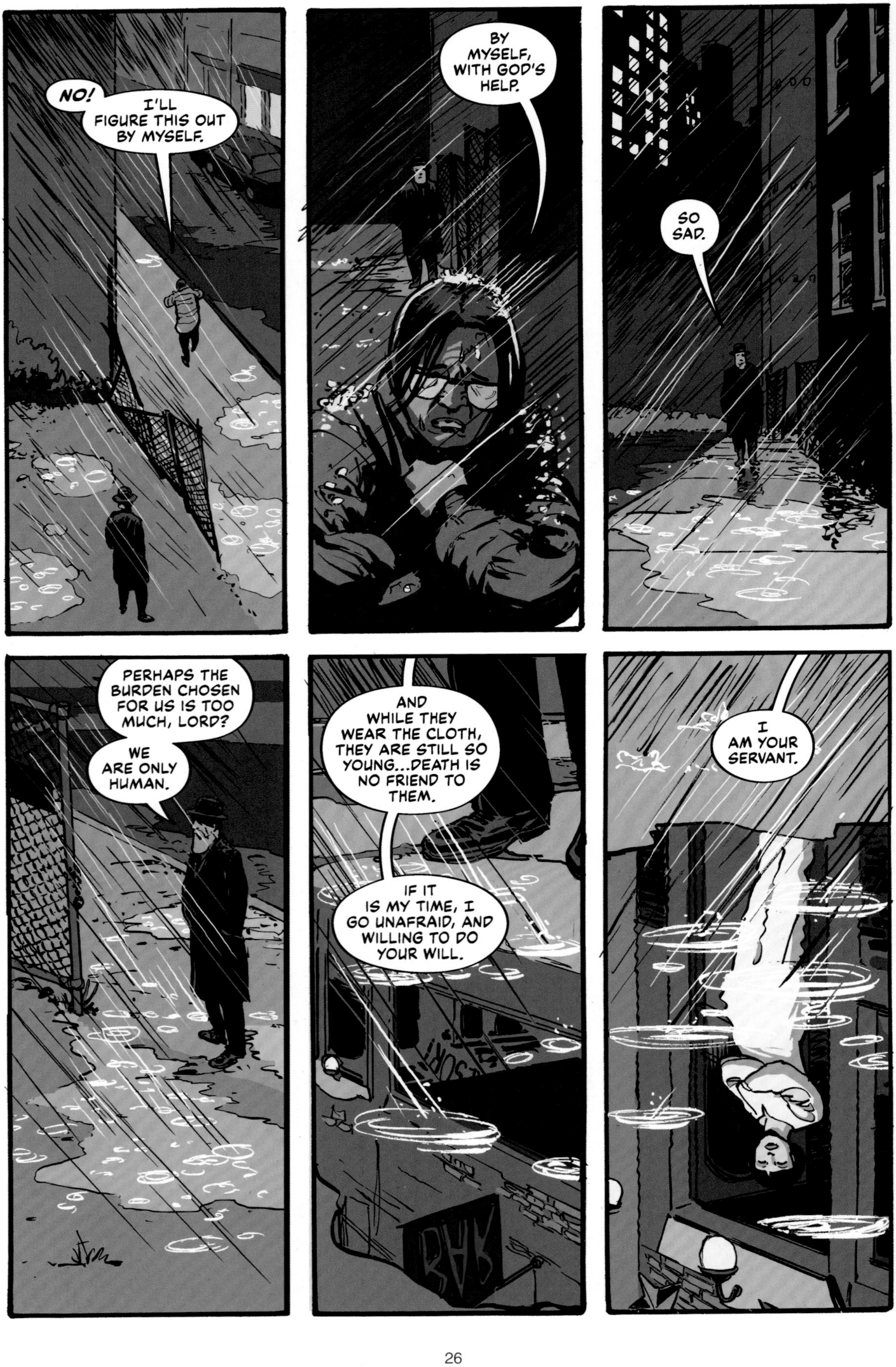
NO!
I'LL FIGURE THIS OUT BY MYSELF.
BY MYSELF, WITH GOD'S HELP.
SO SAD.
PERHAPS THE BURDEN CHOSEN FOR US IS TOO MUCH, LORD?
WE ARE ONLY HUMAN.
AND WHILE THEY WEAR THE CLOTH, THEY ARE STILL SO YOUNG...DEATH IS NO FRIEND TO THEM.
IF IT IS MY TIME, I GO UNAFRAID, AND WILLING TO DO YOUR WILL.
I AM YOUR SERVANT.

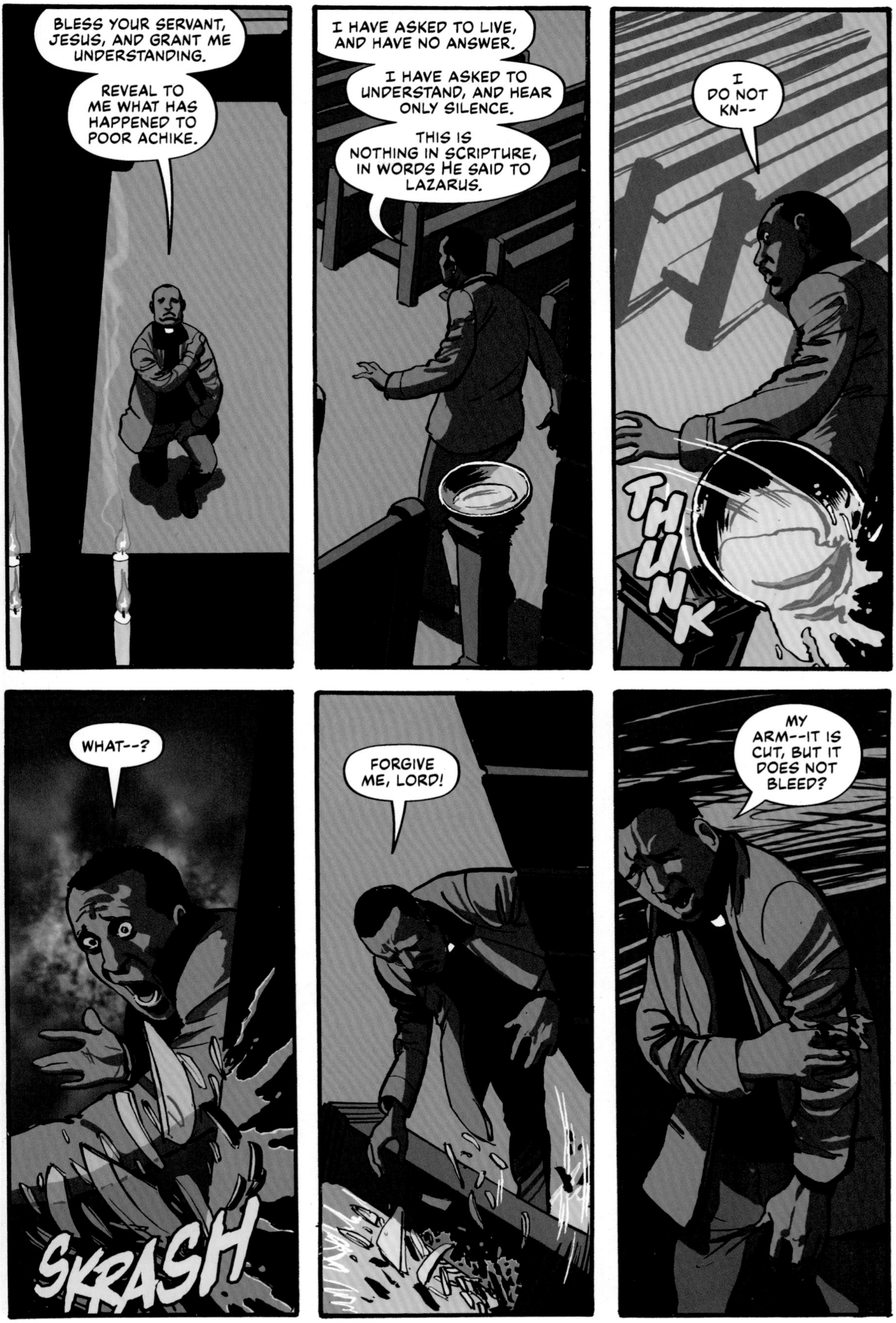
BLESS YOUR SERVANT, JESUS, AND GRANT ME UNDERSTANDING.
REVEAL TO ME WHAT HAS HAPPENED TO POOR ACHIKE.
I HAVE ASKED TO LIVE, AND HAVE NO ANSWER.
I HAVE ASKED TO UNDERSTAND, AND HEAR ONLY SILENCE.
THIS IS NOTHING IN SCRIPTURE, IN WORDS HE SAID TO LAZARUS.
I DO NOT KN--
THUNK
WHAT--?
SKRASH
FORGIVE ME, LORD!
MY ARM--IT IS CUT, BUT IT DOES NOT BLEED?

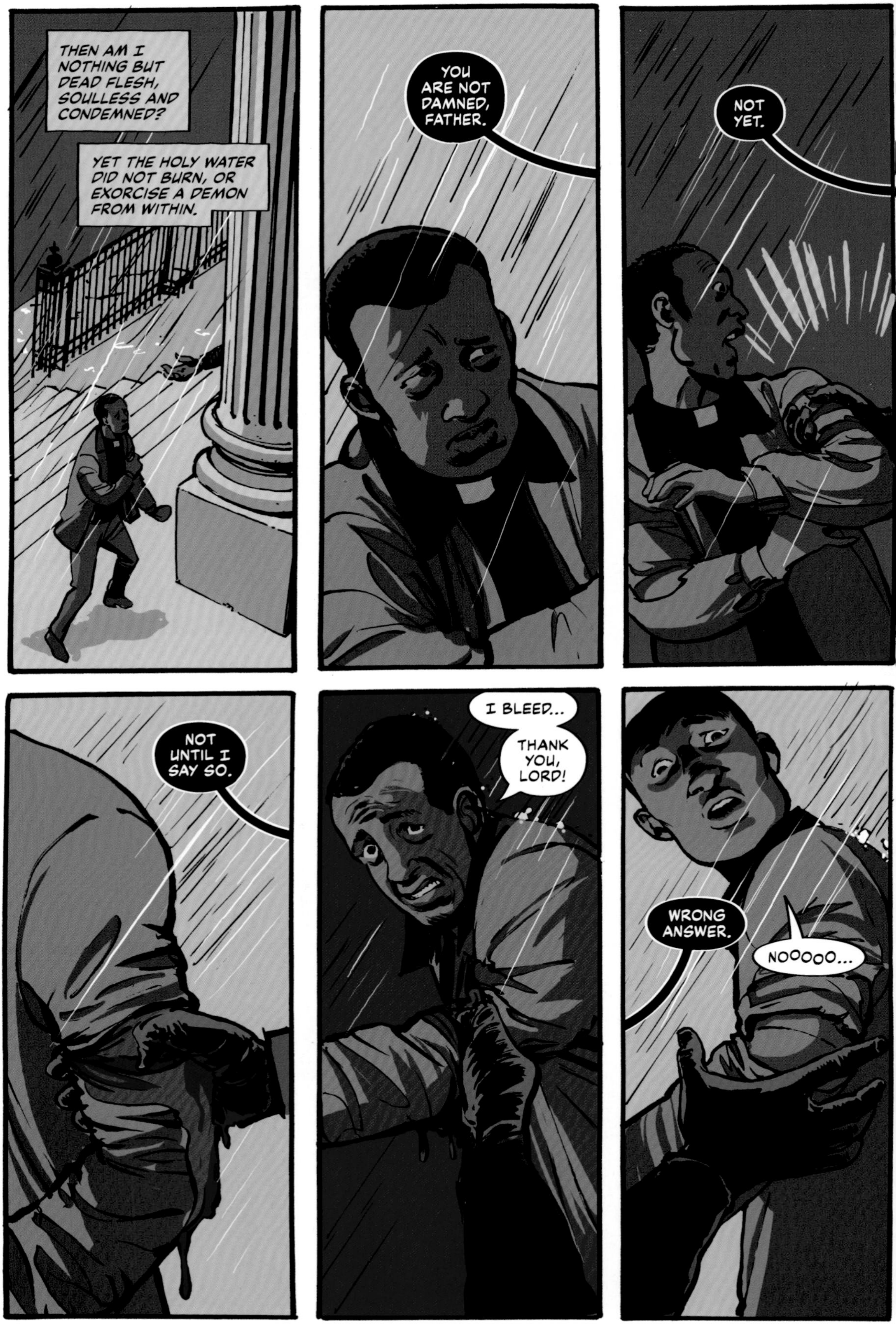
THEN AM I NOTHING BUT DEAD FLESH, SOULLESS AND CONDEMNED?
YET THE HOLY WATER DID NOT BURN, OR EXORCISE A DEMON FROM WITHIN.
YOU ARE NOT DAMNED, FATHER.
NOT YET.
NOT UNTIL I SAY SO.
I BLEED...
THANK YOU, LORD!
WRONG ANSWER.
NOOOOO...

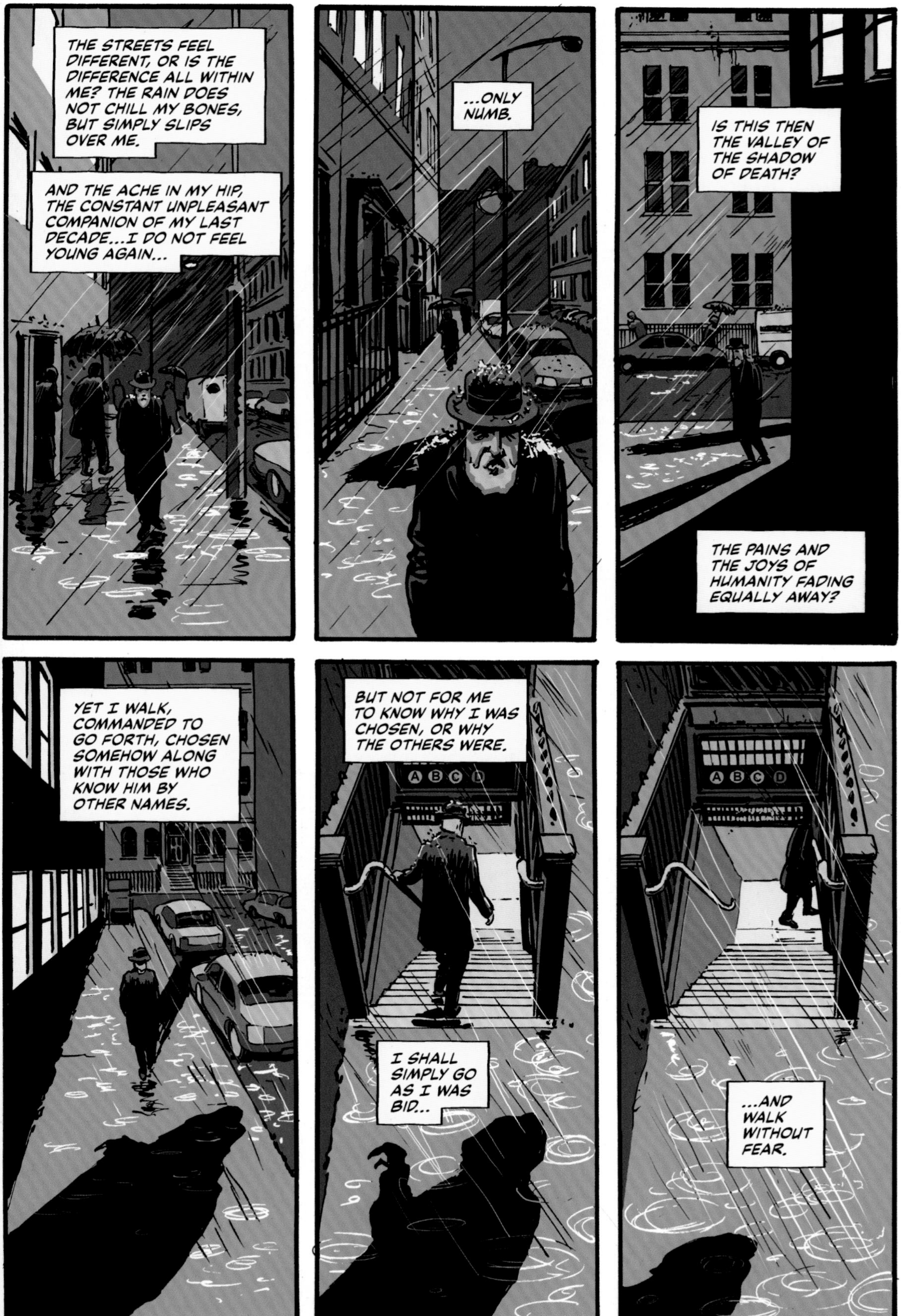
THE STREETS FEEL DIFFERENT, OR IS THE DIFFERENCE ALL WITHIN ME? THE RAIN DOES NOT CHILL MY BONES, BUT SIMPLY SLIPS OVER ME.
AND THE ACHE IN MY HIP, THE CONSTANT UNPLEASANT COMPANION OF MY LAST DECADE...I DO NOT FEEL YOUNG AGAIN...
...ONLY NUMB.
IS THIS THEN THE VALLEY OF THE SHADOW OF DEATH?
THE PAINS AND THE JOYS OF HUMANITY FADING EQUALLY AWAY?
YET I WALK, COMMANDED TO GO FORTH, CHOSEN SOMEHOW ALONG WITH THOSE WHO KNOW HIM BY OTHER NAMES.
BUT NOT FOR ME TO KNOW WHY I WAS CHOSEN, OR WHY THE OTHERS WERE.
A B C D
I SHALL SIMPLY GO AS I WAS BID..
A B C D
...AND WALK WITHOUT FEAR.

I WAS NEVER AFRAID WHEN I WAS HERE... EVERYTHING WAS SIMPLER.

FOLLOW THE FAMILY CALLING, IT'S OPEN TO YOU NOW.

The General Theological Seminary

COULD I BE SAFE THERE AGAIN?

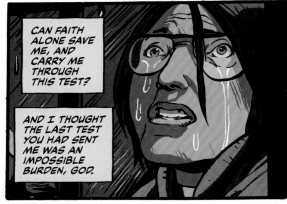

CAN FAITH ALONE SAVE ME, AND CARRY ME THROUGH THIS TEST?

AND I THOUGHT THE LAST TEST YOU HAD SENT ME WAS AN IMPOSSIBLE BURDEN, GOD.

BUT I CAME HERE TO SEE DOCTOR RIFKIN, TO MEET THAT TEST WITH COURAGE AND SAVE THAT MOST PRECIOUS LIFE...

...AND I WILL MEET THIS CHALLENGE TOO, LORD--

--WHETHER I UNDERSTAND IT OR NOT.

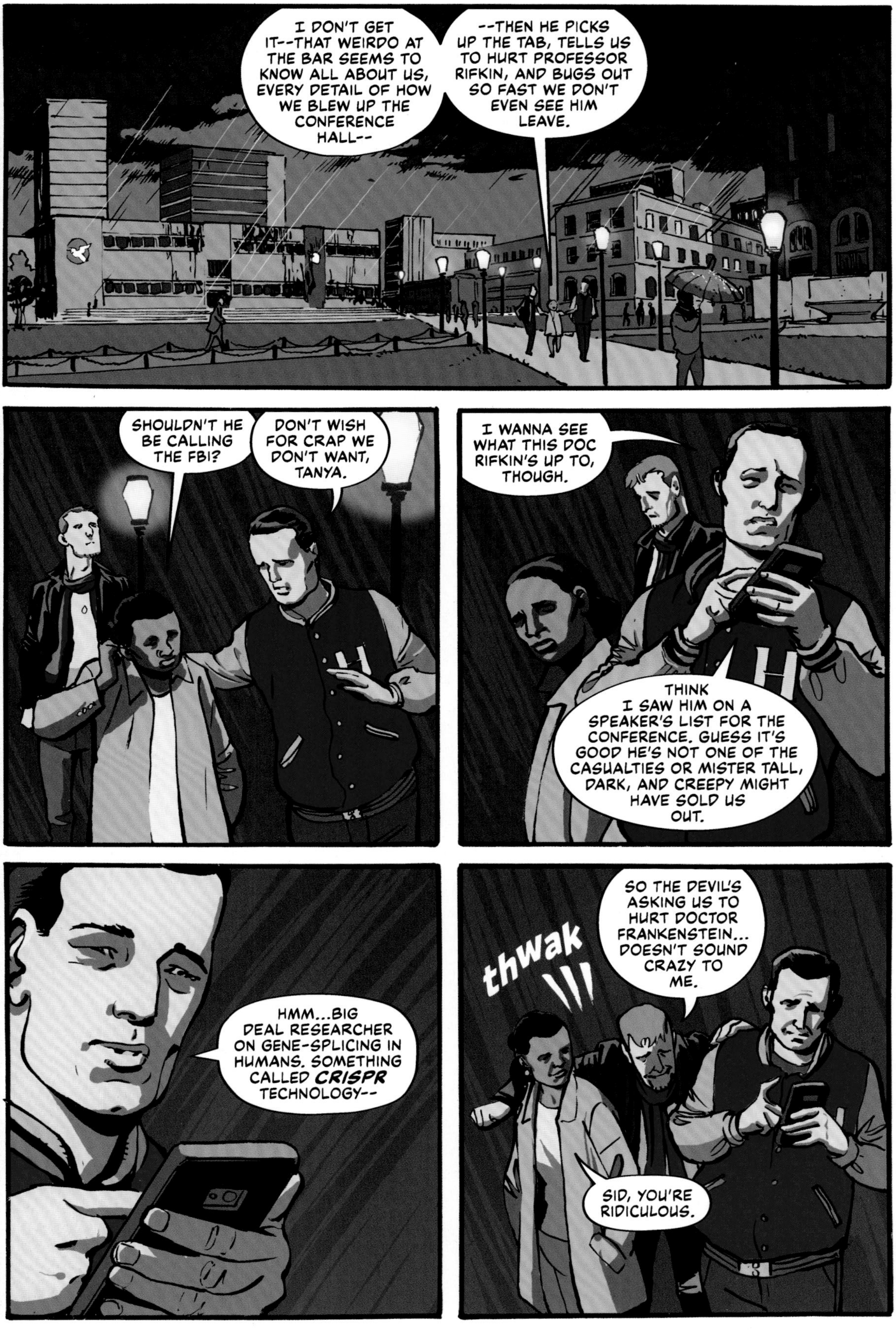
I DON'T GET IT--THAT WEIRDO AT THE BAR SEEMS TO KNOW ALL ABOUT US, EVERY DETAIL OF HOW WE BLEW UP THE CONFERENCE HALL--
--THEN HE PICKS UP THE TAB, TELLS US TO HURT PROFESSOR RIFKIN, AND BUGS OUT SO FAST WE DON'T EVEN SEE HIM LEAVE.
SHOULDN'T HE BE CALLING THE FBI?
DON'T WISH FOR CRAP WE DON'T WANT, TANYA.
I WANNA SEE WHAT THIS DOC RIFKIN'S UP TO, THOUGH.
THINK I SAW HIM ON A SPEAKER'S LIST FOR THE CONFERENCE. GUESS IT'S GOOD HE'S NOT ONE OF THE CASUALTIES OR MISTER TALL, DARK, AND CREEPY MIGHT HAVE SOLD US OUT.
HMM...BIG DEAL RESEARCHER ON GENE-SPLICING IN HUMANS. SOMETHING CALLED *CRISPR* TECHNOLOGY--
thwak
SO THE DEVIL'S ASKING US TO HURT DOCTOR FRANKENSTEIN... DOESN'T SOUND CRAZY TO ME.
SID, YOU'RE RIDICULOUS.

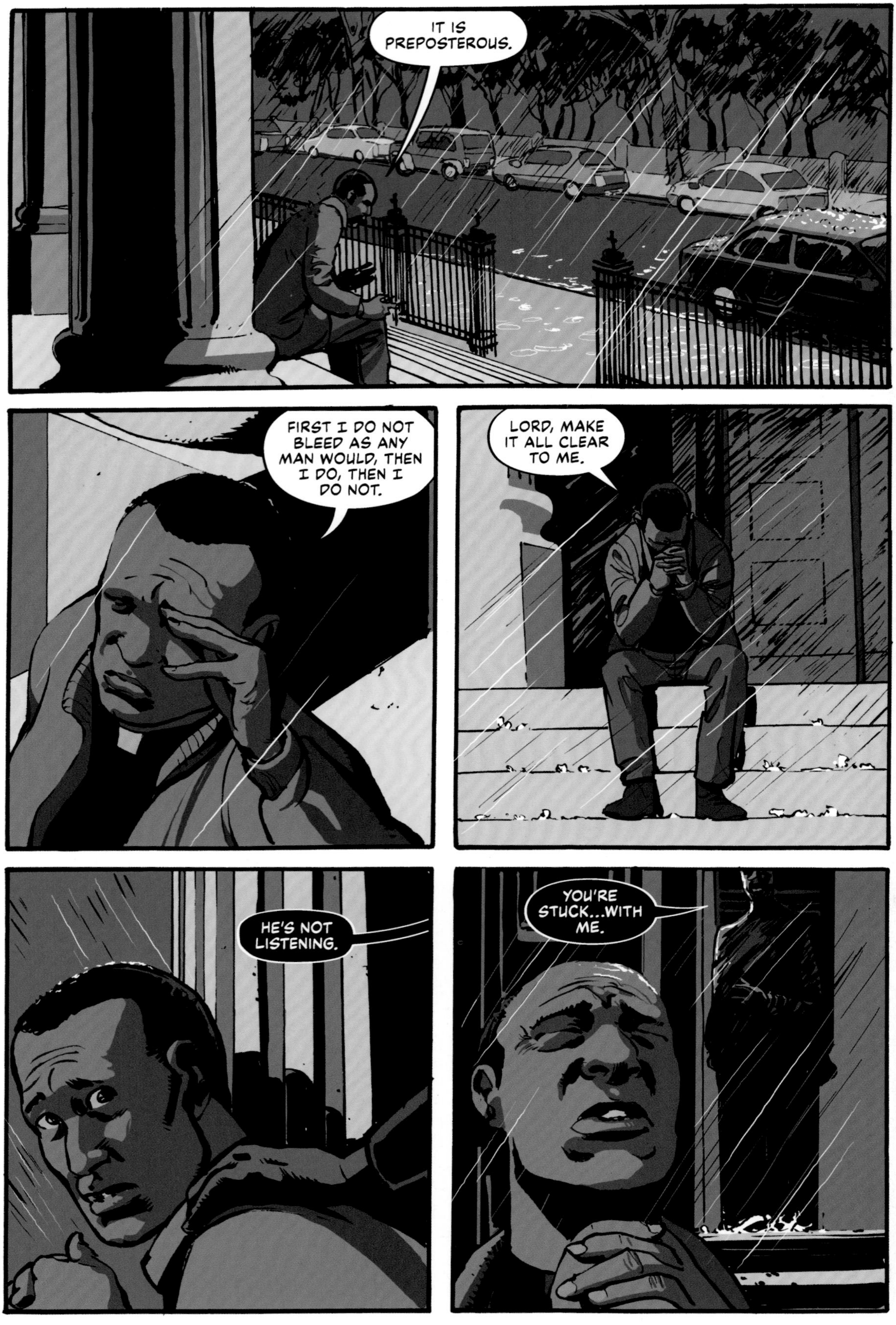
IT IS PREPOSTEROUS.
FIRST I DO NOT BLEED AS ANY MAN WOULD, THEN I DO, THEN I DO NOT.
LORD, MAKE IT ALL CLEAR TO ME.
HE'S NOT LISTENING.
YOU'RE STUCK...WITH ME.

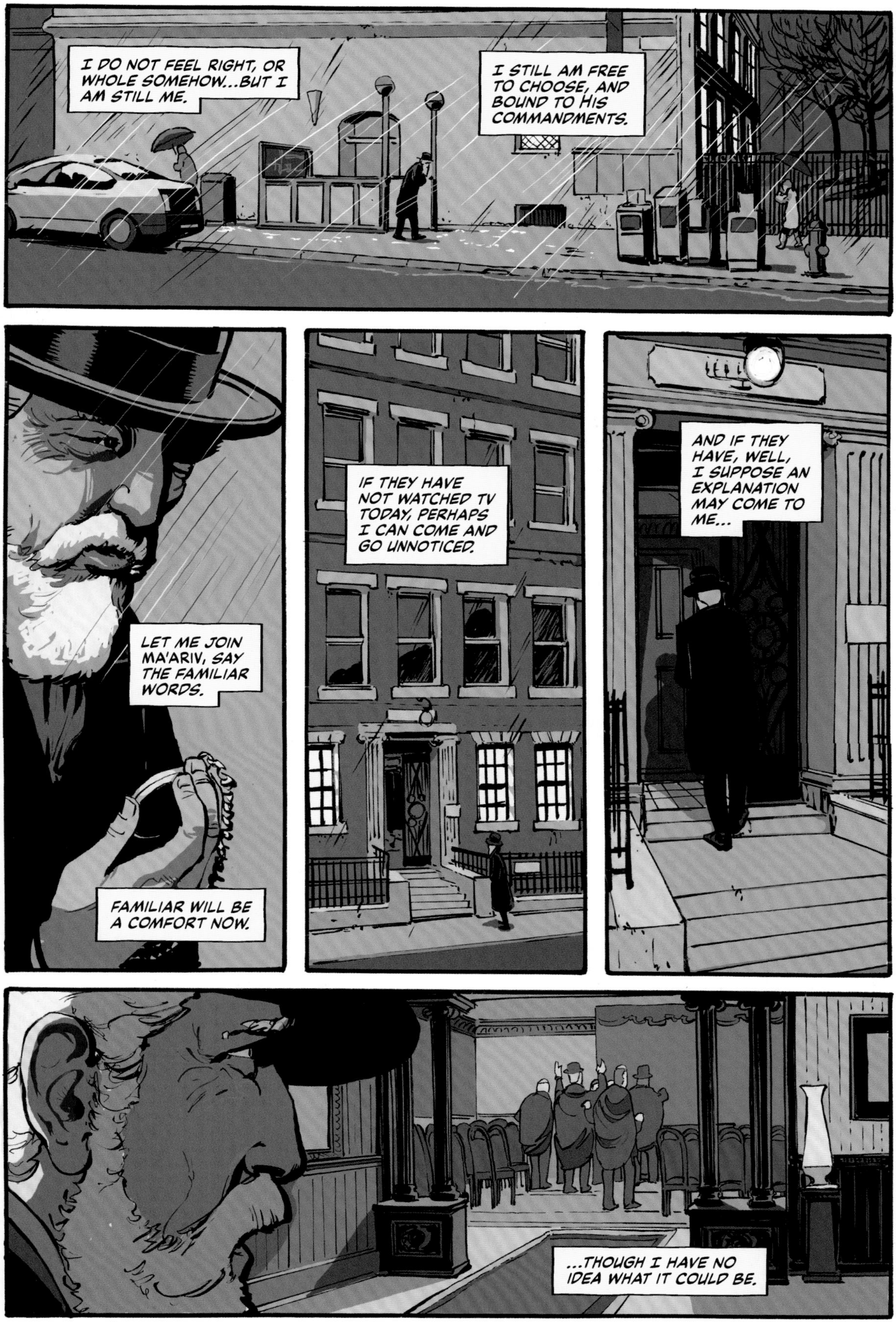
I DO NOT FEEL RIGHT, OR WHOLE SOMEHOW...BUT I AM STILL ME.
I STILL AM FREE TO CHOOSE, AND BOUND TO HIS COMMANDMENTS.
LET ME JOIN MA'ARIV, SAY THE FAMILIAR WORDS.
FAMILIAR WILL BE A COMFORT NOW.
IF THEY HAVE NOT WATCHED TV TODAY, PERHAPS I CAN COME AND GO UNNOTICED.
AND IF THEY HAVE, WELL, I SUPPOSE AN EXPLANATION MAY COME TO ME...
...THOUGH I HAVE NO IDEA WHAT IT COULD BE.

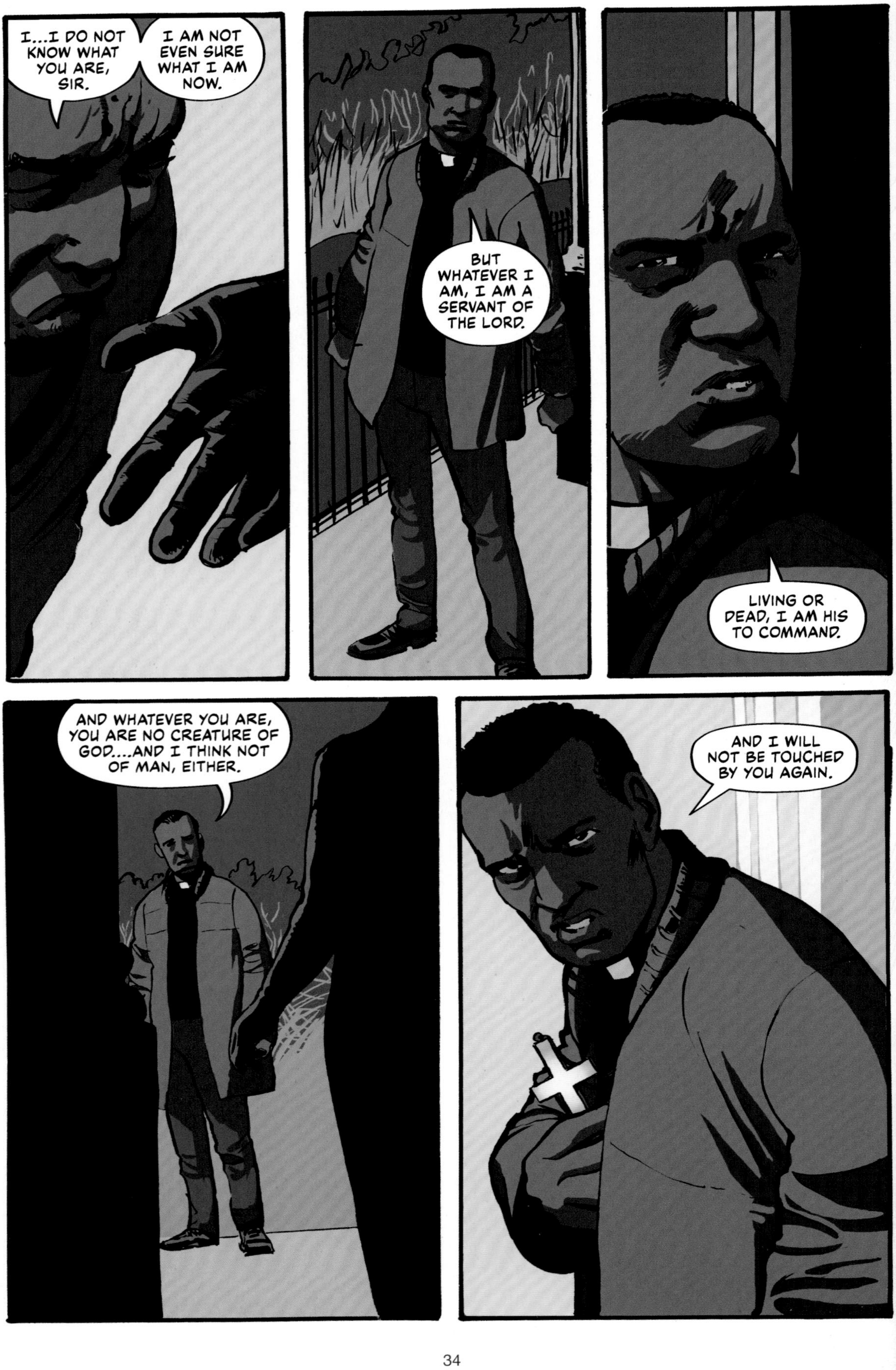

I...I DO NOT KNOW WHAT YOU ARE, SIR.
I AM NOT EVEN SURE WHAT I AM NOW.
BUT WHATEVER I AM, I AM A SERVANT OF THE LORD.
LIVING OR DEAD, I AM HIS TO COMMAND.
AND WHATEVER YOU ARE, YOU ARE NO CREATURE OF GOD....AND I THINK NOT OF MAN, EITHER.
AND I WILL NOT BE TOUCHED BY YOU AGAIN.

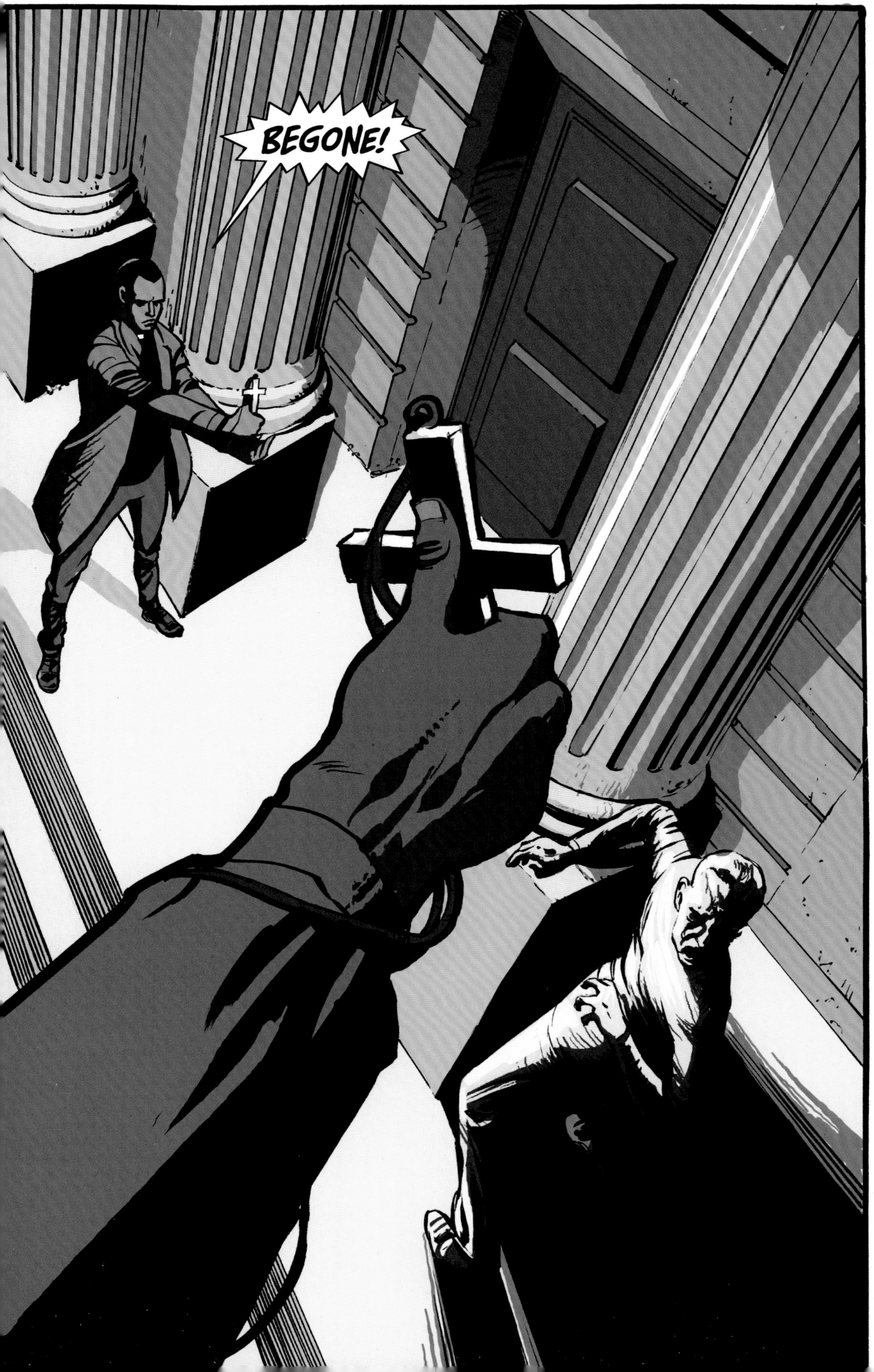
BEGONE!

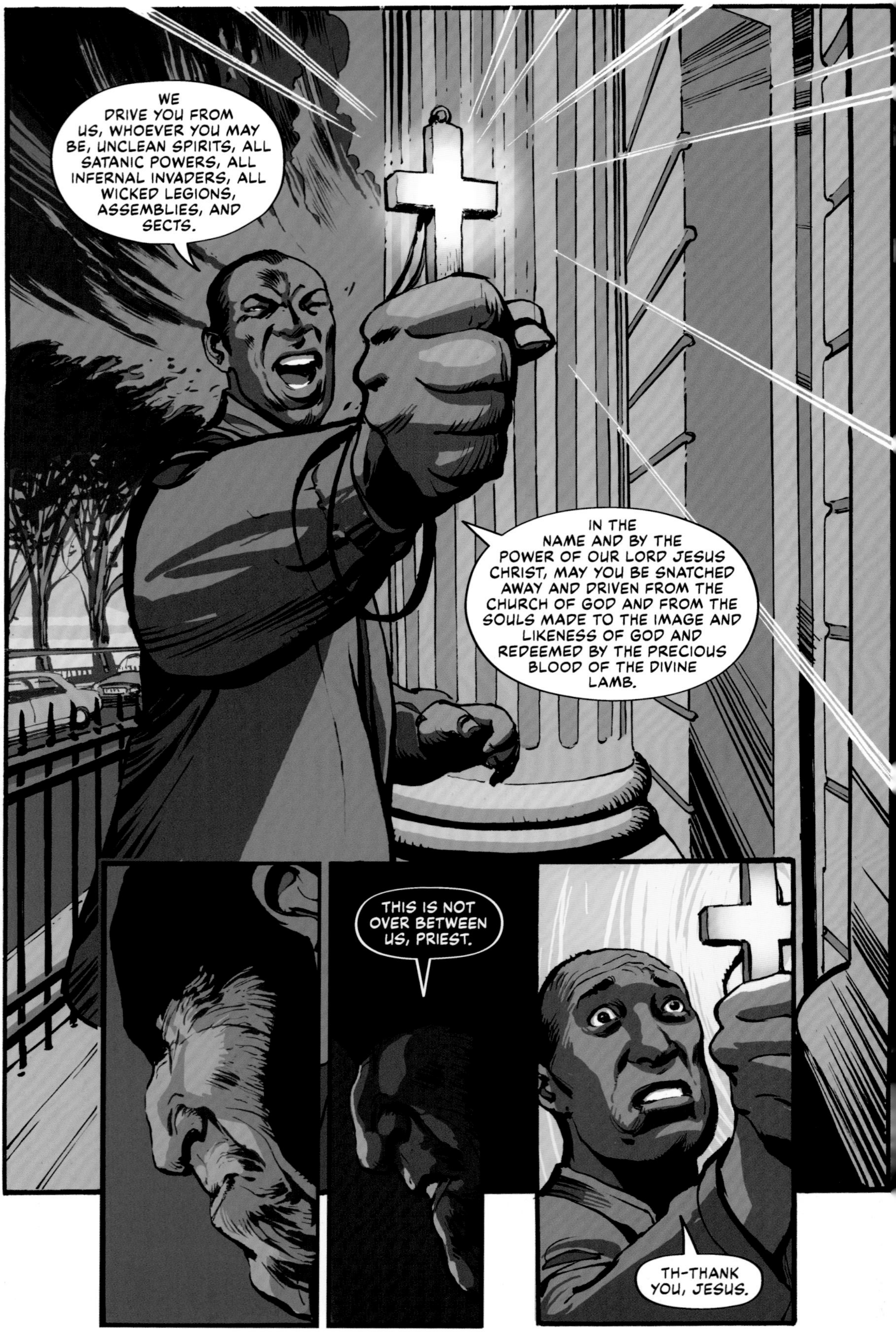
WE DRIVE YOU FROM US, WHOEVER YOU MAY BE, UNCLEAN SPIRITS, ALL SATANIC POWERS, ALL INFERNAL INVADERS, ALL WICKED LEGIONS, ASSEMBLIES, AND SECTS.
IN THE NAME AND BY THE POWER OF OUR LORD JESUS CHRIST, MAY YOU BE SNATCHED AWAY AND DRIVEN FROM THE CHURCH OF GOD AND FROM THE SOULS MADE TO THE IMAGE AND LIKENESS OF GOD AND REDEEMED BY THE PRECIOUS BLOOD OF THE DIVINE LAMB.
THIS IS NOT OVER BETWEEN US, PRIEST.
TH-THANK YOU, JESUS.

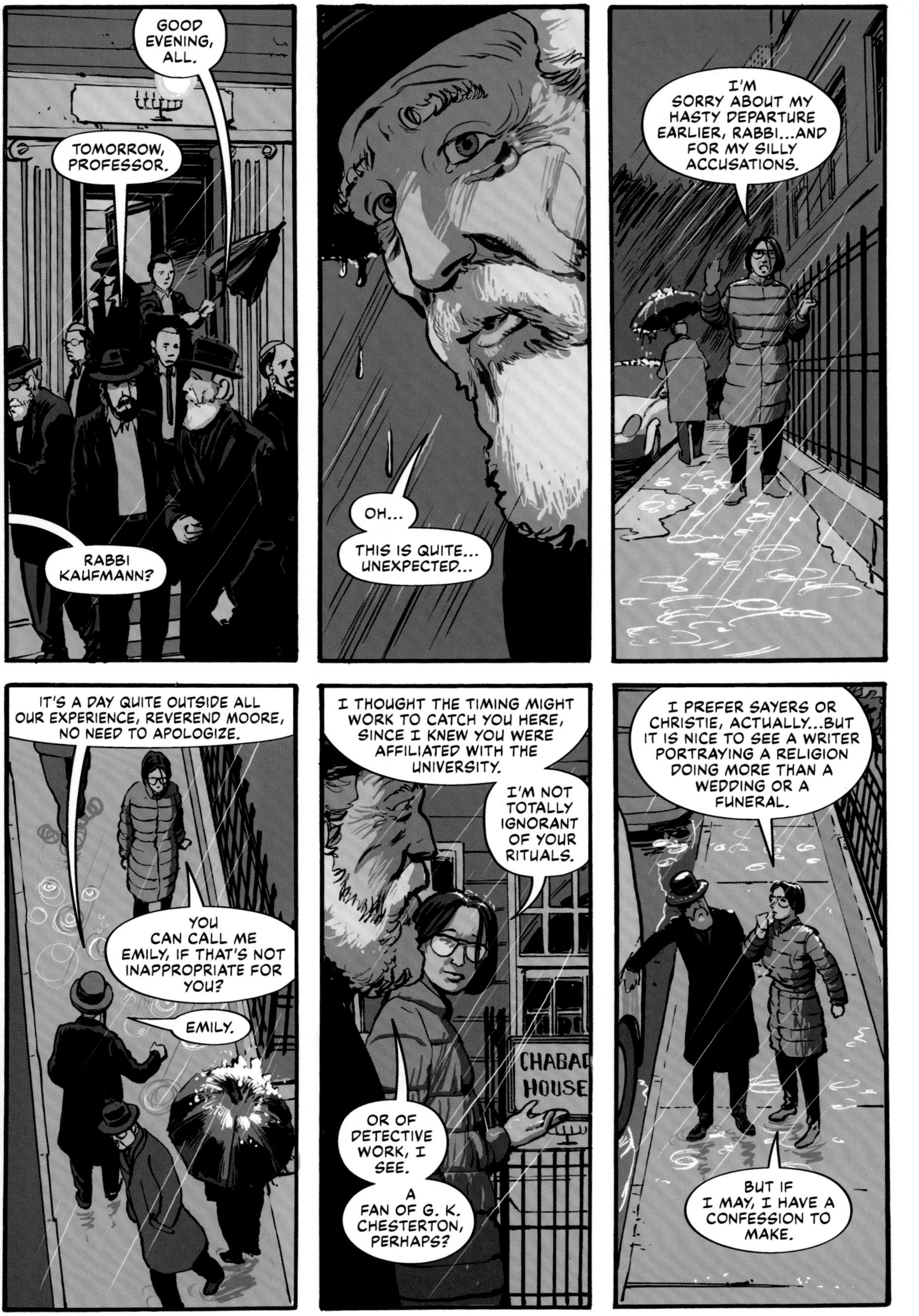
GOOD EVENING, ALL.
TOMORROW, PROFESSOR.
RABBI KAUFMANN?
OH...
THIS IS QUITE... UNEXPECTED...
I'M SORRY ABOUT MY HASTY DEPARTURE EARLIER, RABBI...AND FOR MY SILLY ACCUSATIONS.
IT'S A DAY QUITE OUTSIDE ALL OUR EXPERIENCE, REVEREND MOORE, NO NEED TO APOLOGIZE.
YOU CAN CALL ME EMILY, IF THAT'S NOT INAPPROPRIATE FOR YOU?
EMILY.
I THOUGHT THE TIMING MIGHT WORK TO CATCH YOU HERE, SINCE I KNEW YOU WERE AFFILIATED WITH THE UNIVERSITY.
I'M NOT TOTALLY IGNORANT OF YOUR RITUALS.
CHABAD HOUSE
OR OF DETECTIVE WORK, I SEE.
A FAN OF G. K. CHESTERTON, PERHAPS?
I PREFER SAYERS OR CHRISTIE, ACTUALLY...BUT IT IS NICE TO SEE A WRITER PORTRAYING A RELIGION DOING MORE THAN A WEDDING OR A FUNERAL.
BUT IF I MAY, I HAVE A CONFESSION TO MAKE.

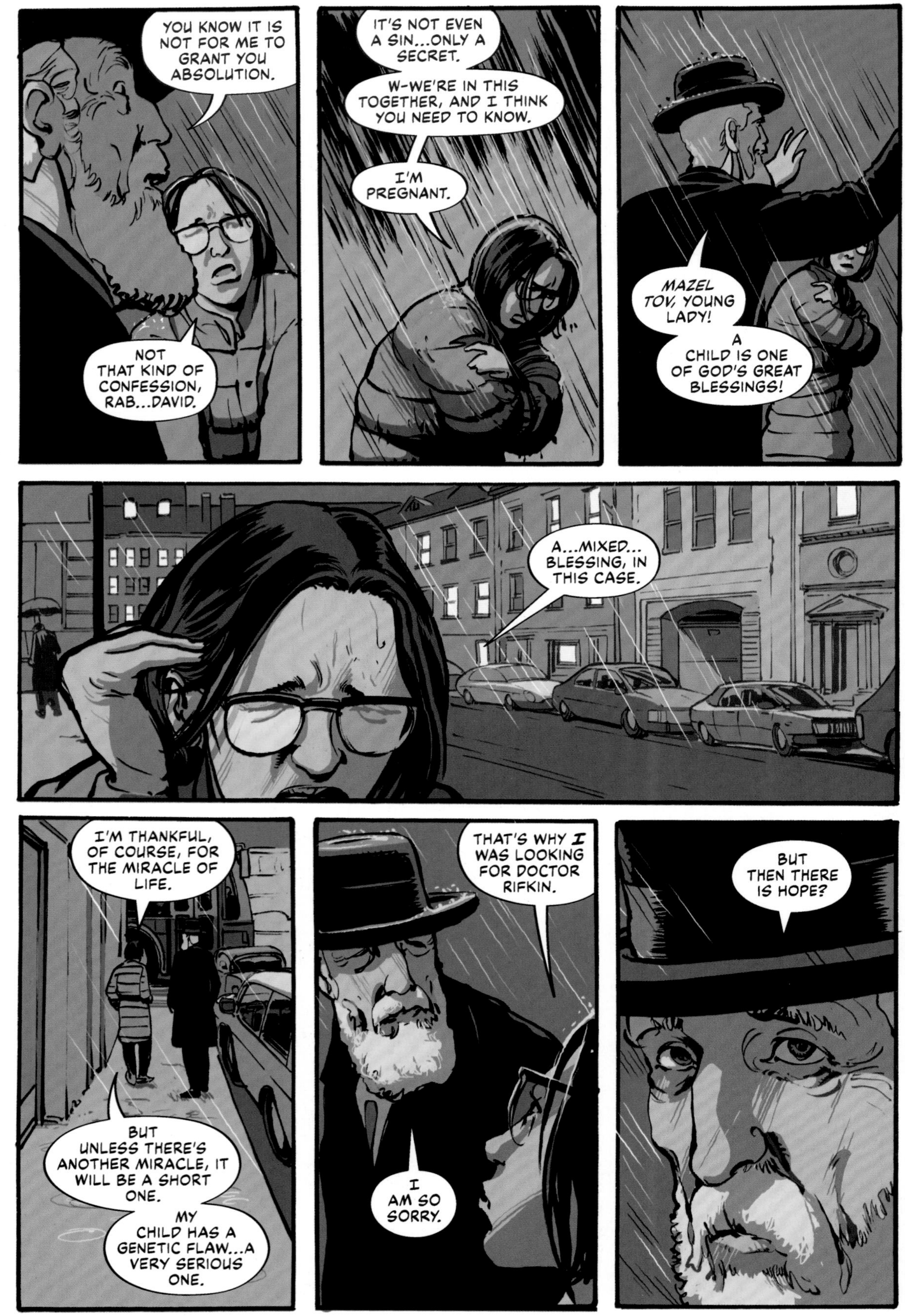
YOU KNOW IT IS NOT FOR ME TO GRANT YOU ABSOLUTION.
NOT THAT KIND OF CONFESSION, RAB...DAVID.
IT'S NOT EVEN A SIN...ONLY A SECRET.
W-WE'RE IN THIS TOGETHER, AND I THINK YOU NEED TO KNOW.
I'M PREGNANT.
MAZEL TOV, YOUNG LADY!
A CHILD IS ONE OF GOD'S GREAT BLESSINGS!
A...MIXED... BLESSING, IN THIS CASE.
I'M THANKFUL, OF COURSE, FOR THE MIRACLE OF LIFE.
BUT UNLESS THERE'S ANOTHER MIRACLE, IT WILL BE A SHORT ONE.
MY CHILD HAS A GENETIC FLAW...A VERY SERIOUS ONE.
THAT'S WHY I WAS LOOKING FOR DOCTOR RIFKIN.
I AM SO SORRY.
BUT THEN THERE IS HOPE?

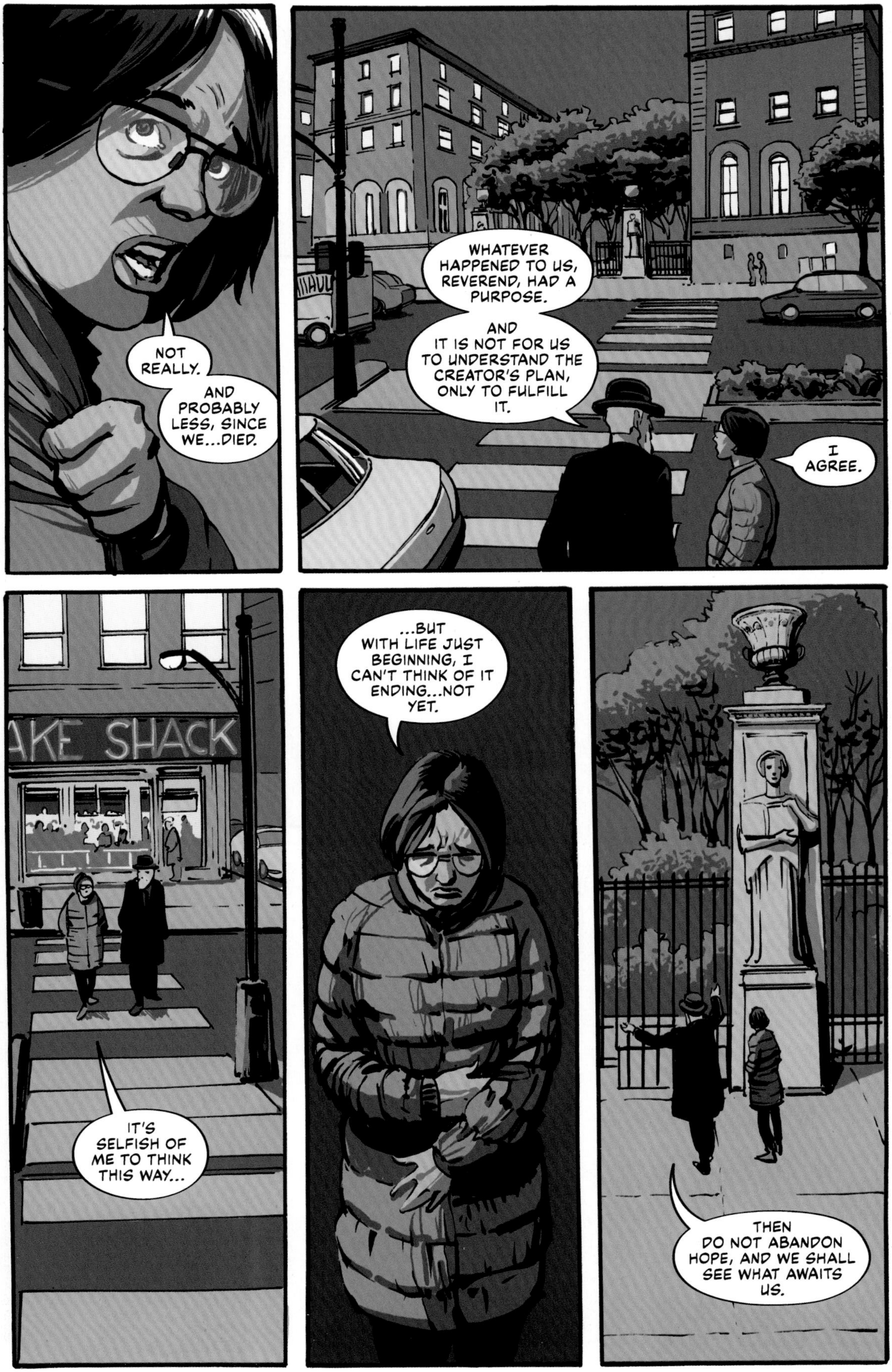
NOT REALLY.
AND PROBABLY LESS, SINCE WE...DIED.
WHATEVER HAPPENED TO US, REVEREND, HAD A PURPOSE.
AND IT IS NOT FOR US TO UNDERSTAND THE CREATOR'S PLAN, ONLY TO FULFILL IT.
I AGREE.
AKE SHACK
IT'S SELFISH OF ME TO THINK THIS WAY...
...BUT WITH LIFE JUST BEGINNING, I CAN'T THINK OF IT ENDING...NOT YET.
THEN DO NOT ABANDON HOPE, AND WE SHALL SEE WHAT AWAITS US.

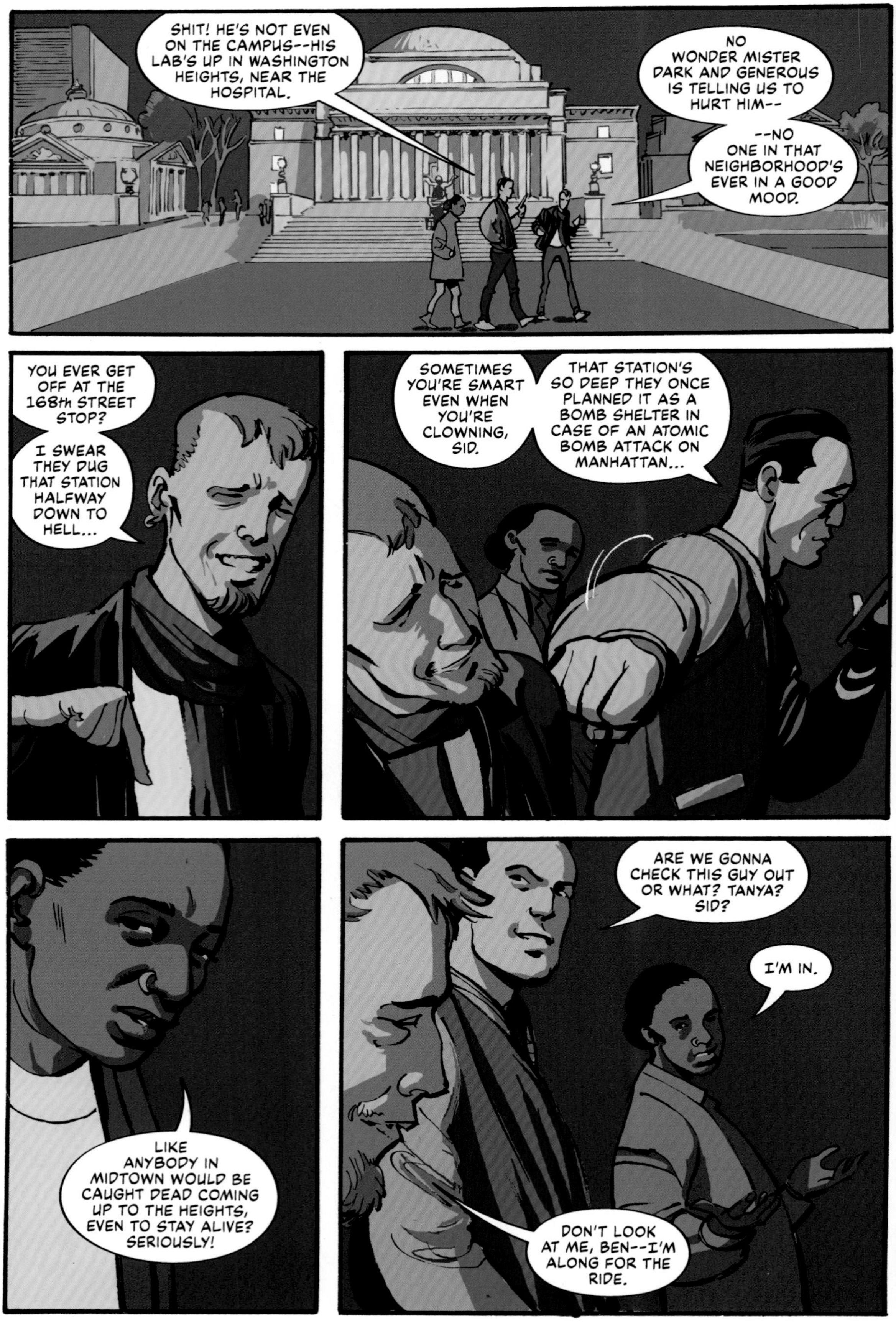
SHIT! HE'S NOT EVEN ON THE CAMPUS--HIS LAB'S UP IN WASHINGTON HEIGHTS, NEAR THE HOSPITAL.
NO WONDER MISTER DARK AND GENEROUS IS TELLING US TO HURT HIM--
--NO ONE IN THAT NEIGHBORHOOD'S EVER IN A GOOD MOOD.
YOU EVER GET OFF AT THE 168th STREET STOP?
I SWEAR THEY DUG THAT STATION HALFWAY DOWN TO HELL...
SOMETIMES YOU'RE SMART EVEN WHEN YOU'RE CLOWNING, SID.
THAT STATION'S SO DEEP THEY ONCE PLANNED IT AS A BOMB SHELTER IN CASE OF AN ATOMIC BOMB ATTACK ON MANHATTAN...
LIKE ANYBODY IN MIDTOWN WOULD BE CAUGHT DEAD COMING UP TO THE HEIGHTS, EVEN TO STAY ALIVE? SERIOUSLY!
ARE WE GONNA CHECK THIS GUY OUT OR WHAT? TANYA? SID?
I'M IN.
DON'T LOOK AT ME, BEN--I'M ALONG FOR THE RIDE.

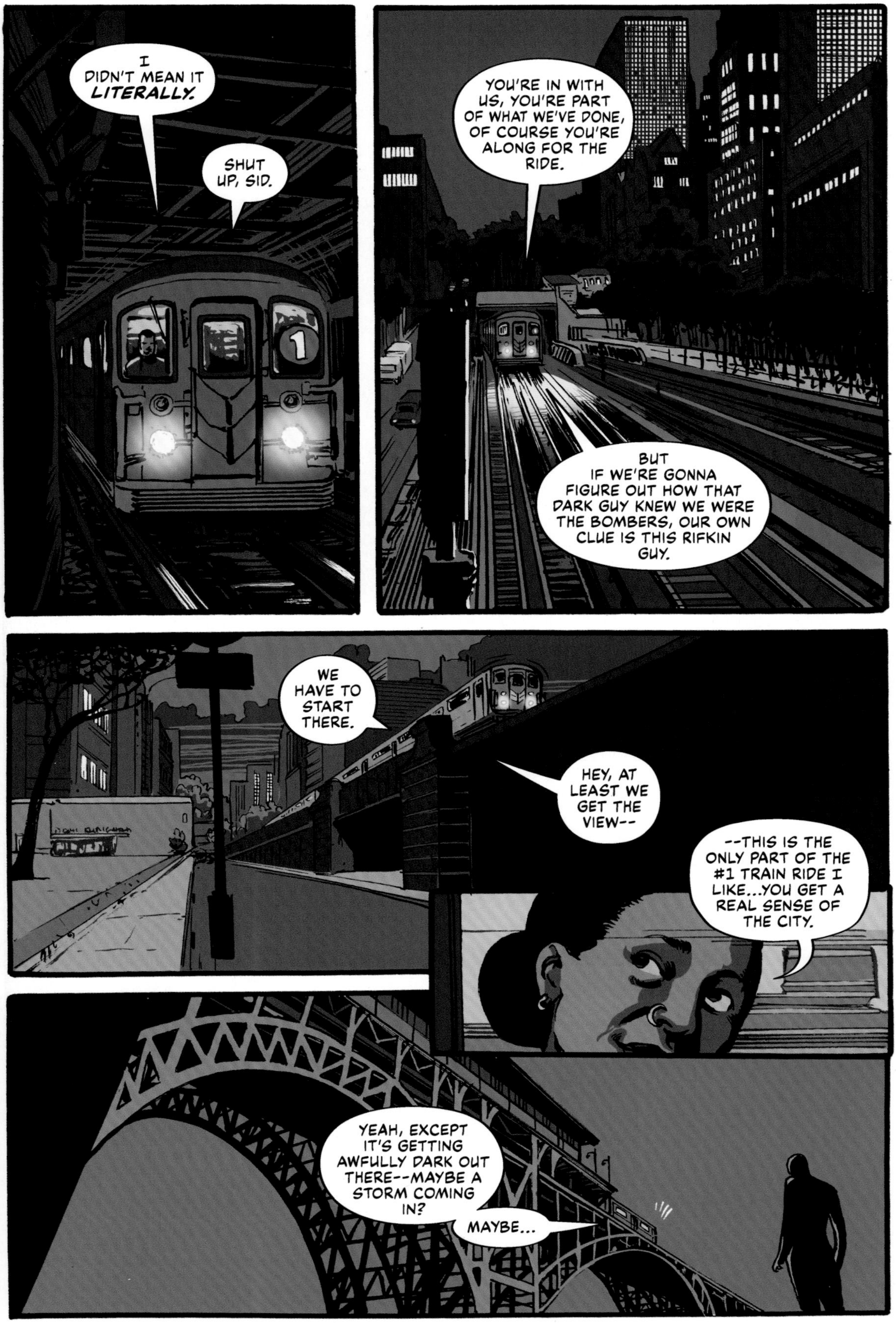
I DIDN'T MEAN IT LITERALLY.
SHUT UP, SID.
YOU'RE IN WITH US, YOU'RE PART OF WHAT WE'VE DONE, OF COURSE YOU'RE ALONG FOR THE RIDE.
BUT IF WE'RE GONNA FIGURE OUT HOW THAT DARK GUY KNEW WE WERE THE BOMBERS, OUR OWN CLUE IS THIS RIFKIN GUY.
WE HAVE TO START THERE.
HEY, AT LEAST WE GET THE VIEW--
--THIS IS THE ONLY PART OF THE #1 TRAIN RIDE I LIKE...YOU GET A REAL SENSE OF THE CITY.
YEAH, EXCEPT IT'S GETTING AWFULLY DARK OUT THERE--MAYBE A STORM COMING IN?
MAYBE...

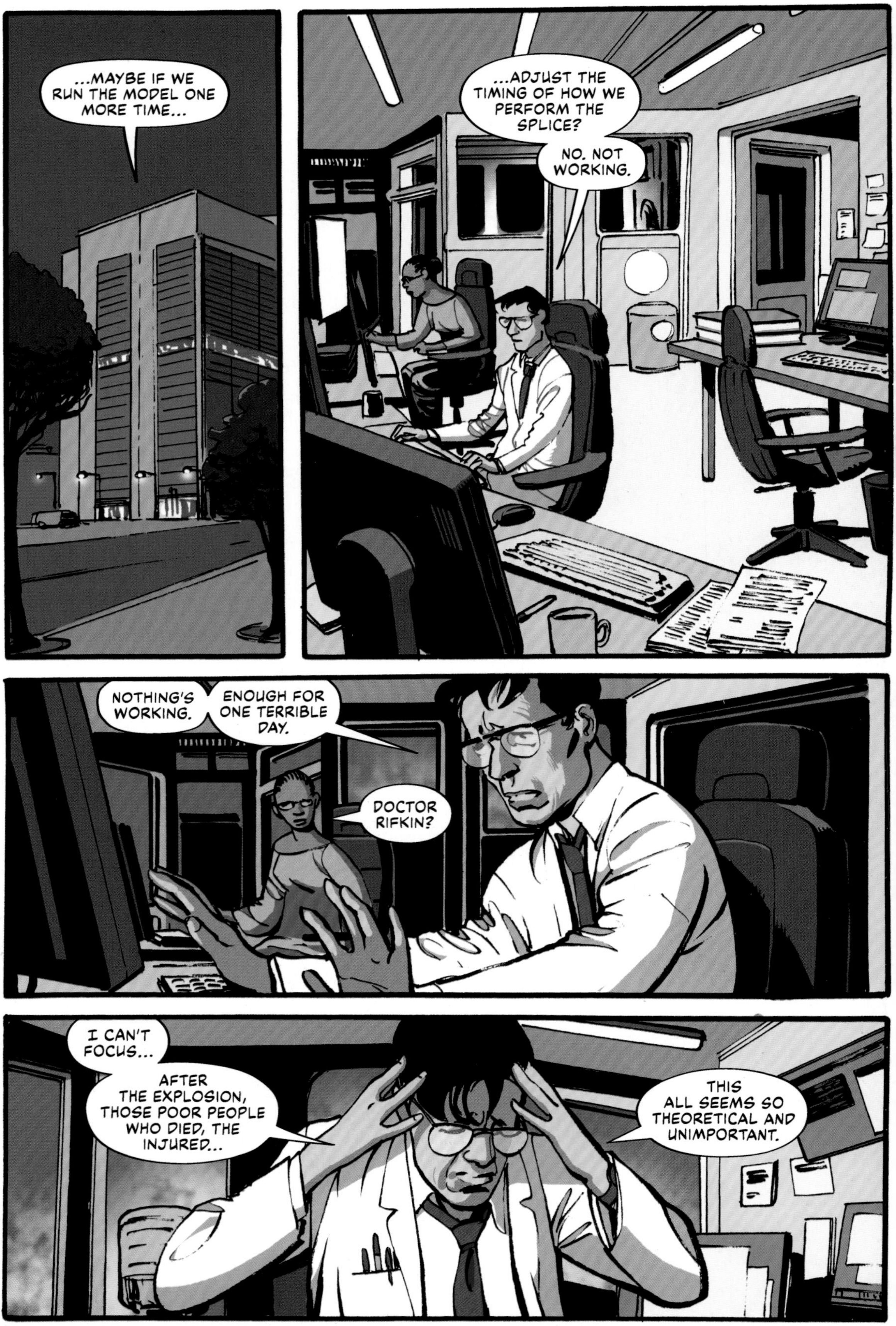
...MAYBE IF WE RUN THE MODEL ONE MORE TIME...
...ADJUST THE TIMING OF HOW WE PERFORM THE SPLICE?
NO. NOT WORKING.
NOTHING'S WORKING.
ENOUGH FOR ONE TERRIBLE DAY.
DOCTOR RIFKIN?
I CAN'T FOCUS...
AFTER THE EXPLOSION, THOSE POOR PEOPLE WHO DIED, THE INJURED...
THIS ALL SEEMS SO THEORETICAL AND UNIMPORTANT.

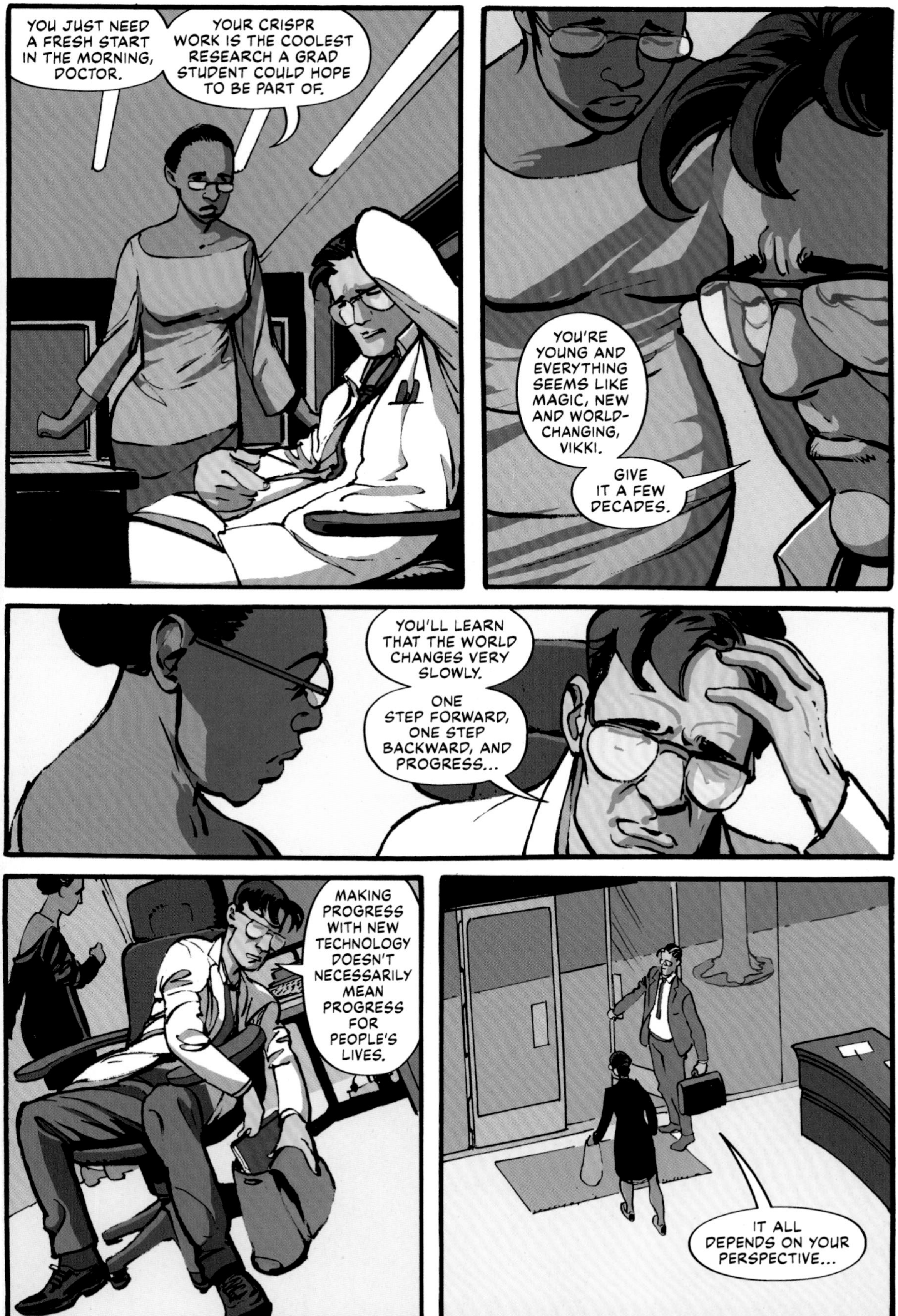
YOU JUST NEED A FRESH START IN THE MORNING, DOCTOR.
YOUR CRISPR WORK IS THE COOLEST RESEARCH A GRAD STUDENT COULD HOPE TO BE PART OF.
YOU'RE YOUNG AND EVERYTHING SEEMS LIKE MAGIC, NEW AND WORLD-CHANGING, VIKKI.
GIVE IT A FEW DECADES.
YOU'LL LEARN THAT THE WORLD CHANGES VERY SLOWLY.
ONE STEP FORWARD, ONE STEP BACKWARD, AND PROGRESS...
MAKING PROGRESS WITH NEW TECHNOLOGY DOESN'T NECESSARILY MEAN PROGRESS FOR PEOPLE'S LIVES.
IT ALL DEPENDS ON YOUR PERSPECTIVE...

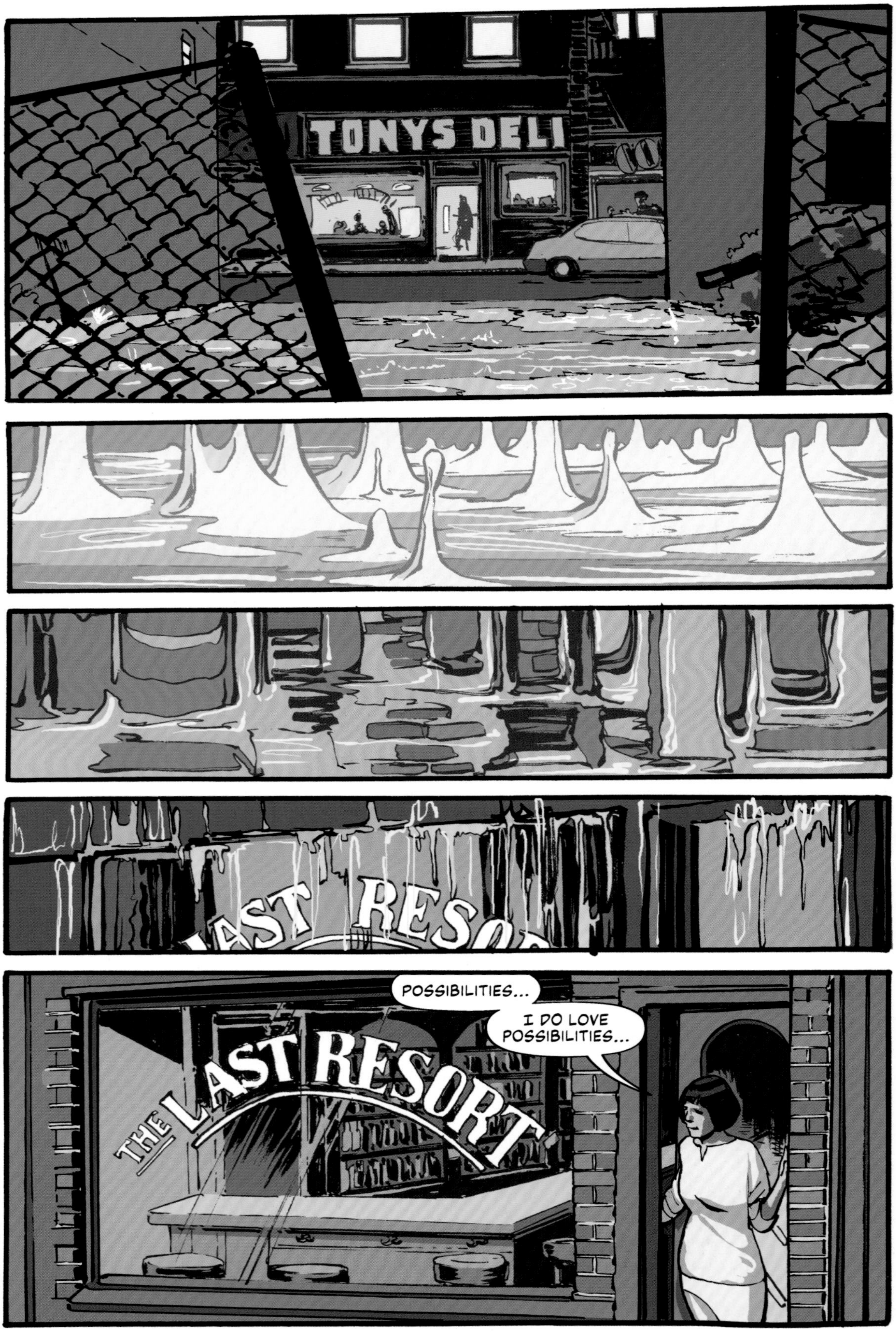
TONYS DELI
LAST RESO
POSSIBILITIES...
I DO LOVE POSSIBILITIES...
THE LAST RESORT

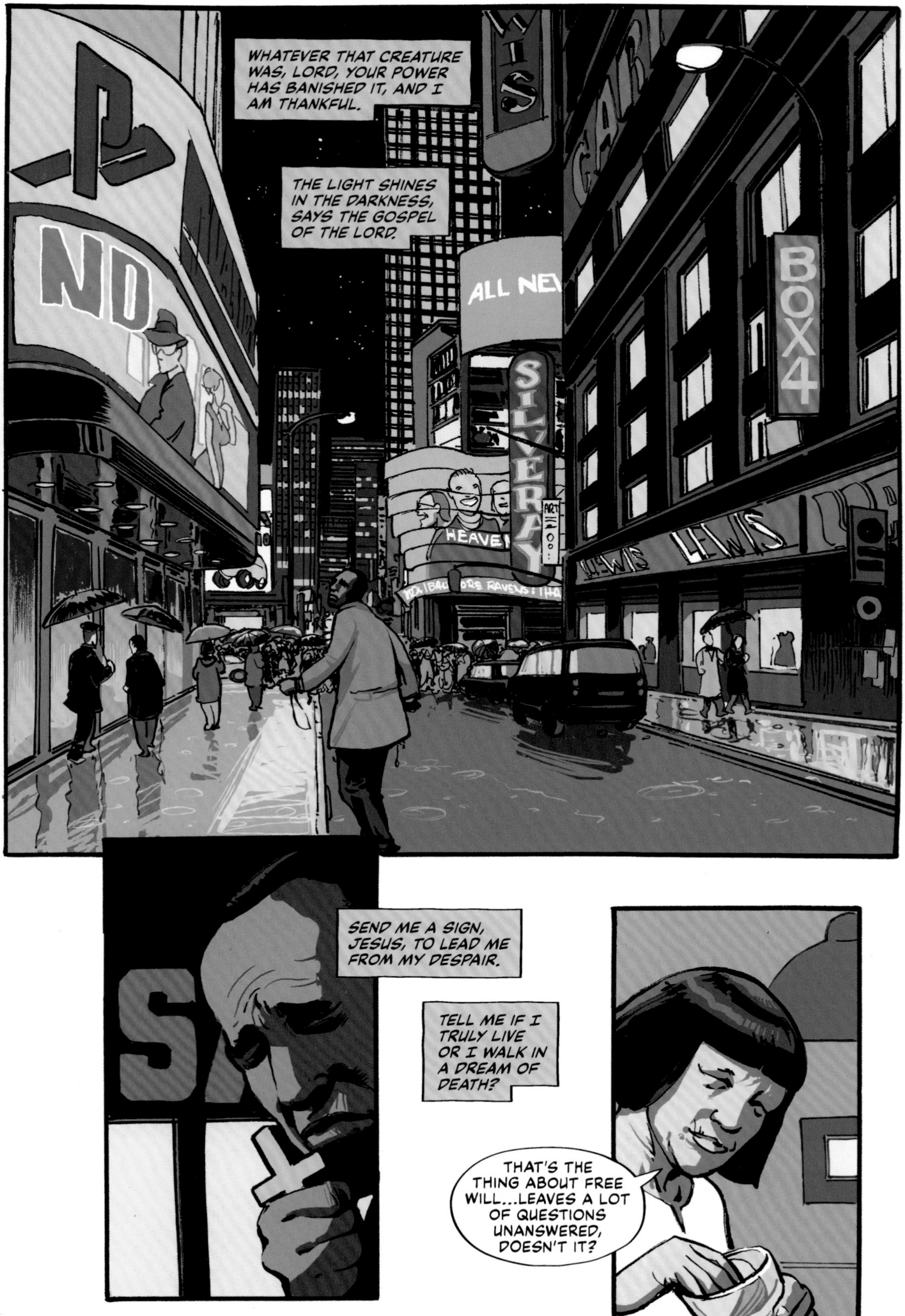
WHATEVER THAT CREATURE WAS, LORD, YOUR POWER HAS BANISHED IT, AND I AM THANKFUL.
THE LIGHT SHINES IN THE DARKNESS, SAYS THE GOSPEL OF THE LORD.
ALL NEW
SILVERAY
BOX4
HEAVEN
LEWIS
SEND ME A SIGN, JESUS, TO LEAD ME FROM MY DESPAIR.
TELL ME IF I TRULY LIVE OR I WALK IN A DREAM OF DEATH?
THAT'S THE THING ABOUT FREE WILL...LEAVES A LOT OF QUESTIONS UNANSWERED, DOESN'T IT?

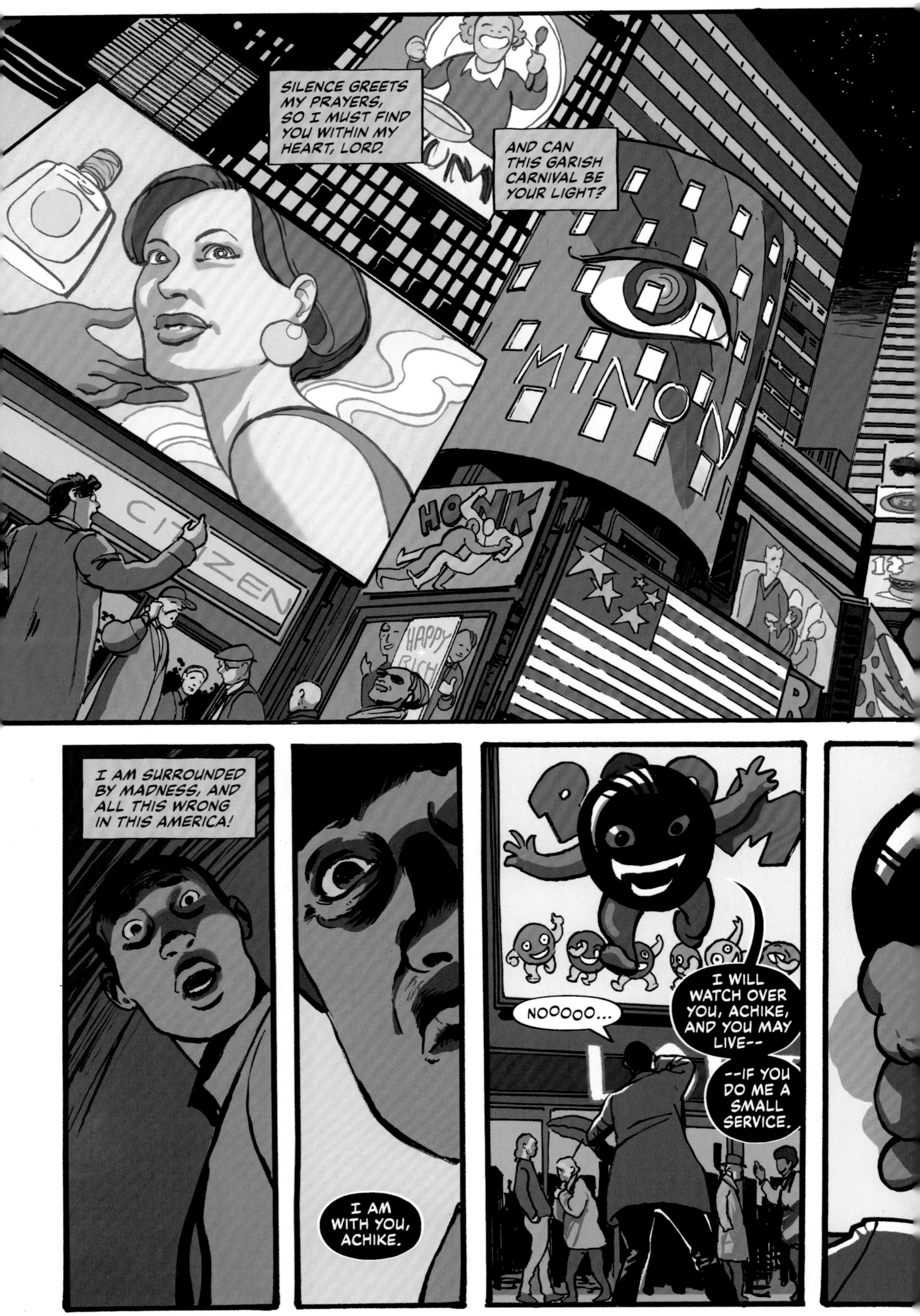

SILENCE GREETS MY PRAYERS, SO I MUST FIND YOU WITHIN MY HEART, LORD.
AND CAN THIS GARISH CARNIVAL BE YOUR LIGHT?
MINON
HONK
CITIZEN
HAPPY RICH
I AM SURROUNDED BY MADNESS, AND ALL THIS WRONG IN THIS AMERICA!
I AM WITH YOU, ACHIKE.
NOOOOO...
I WILL WATCH OVER YOU, ACHIKE, AND YOU MAY LIVE--
--IF YOU DO ME A SMALL SERVICE.

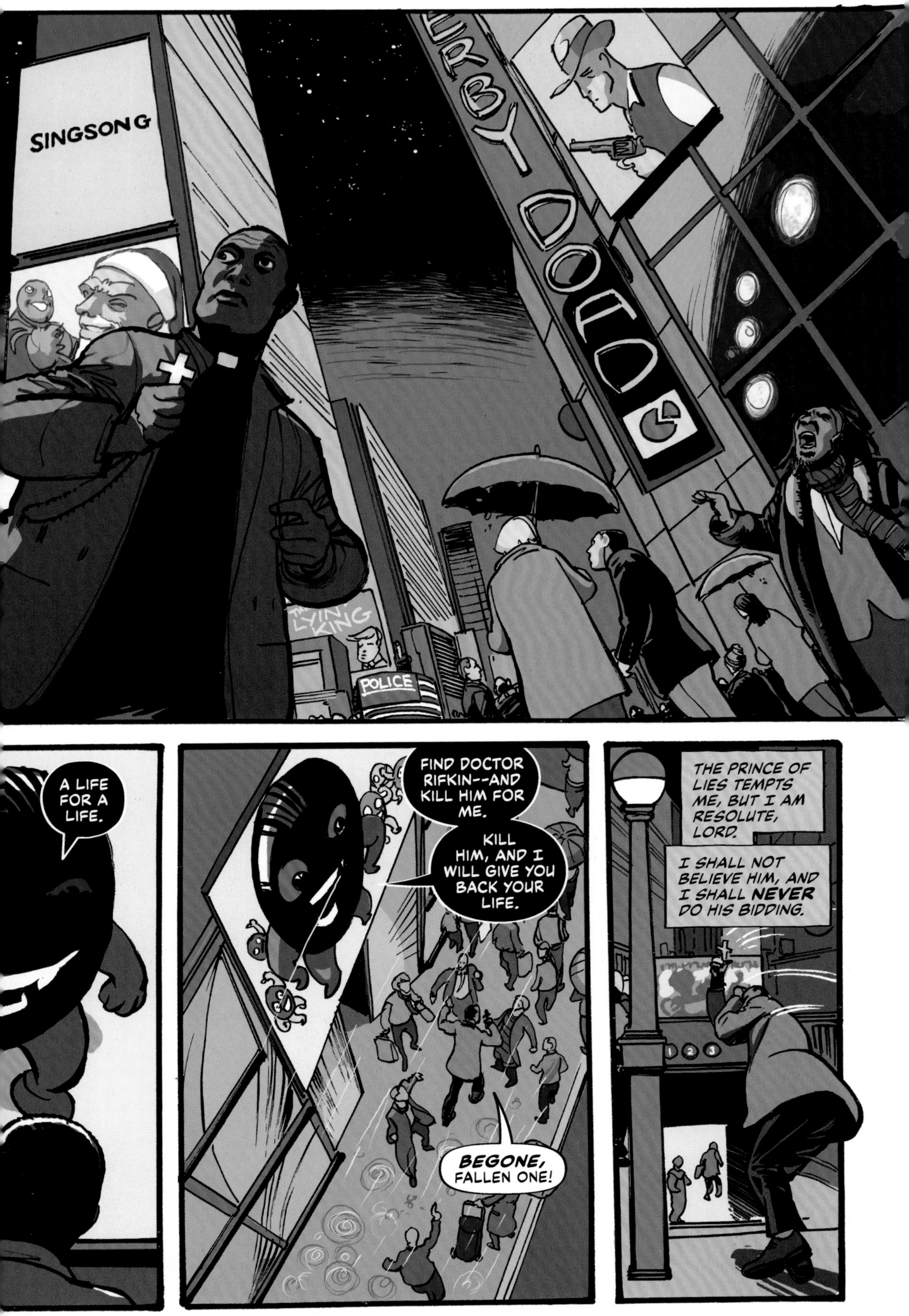
SINGSONG
DERBY DOAD
THE LYING KING
POLICE
A LIFE FOR A LIFE.
FIND DOCTOR RIFKIN--AND KILL HIM FOR ME.
KILL HIM, AND I WILL GIVE YOU BACK YOUR LIFE.
BEGONE, FALLEN ONE!
THE PRINCE OF LIES TEMPTS ME, BUT I AM RESOLUTE, LORD.
I SHALL NOT BELIEVE HIM, AND I SHALL NEVER DO HIS BIDDING.

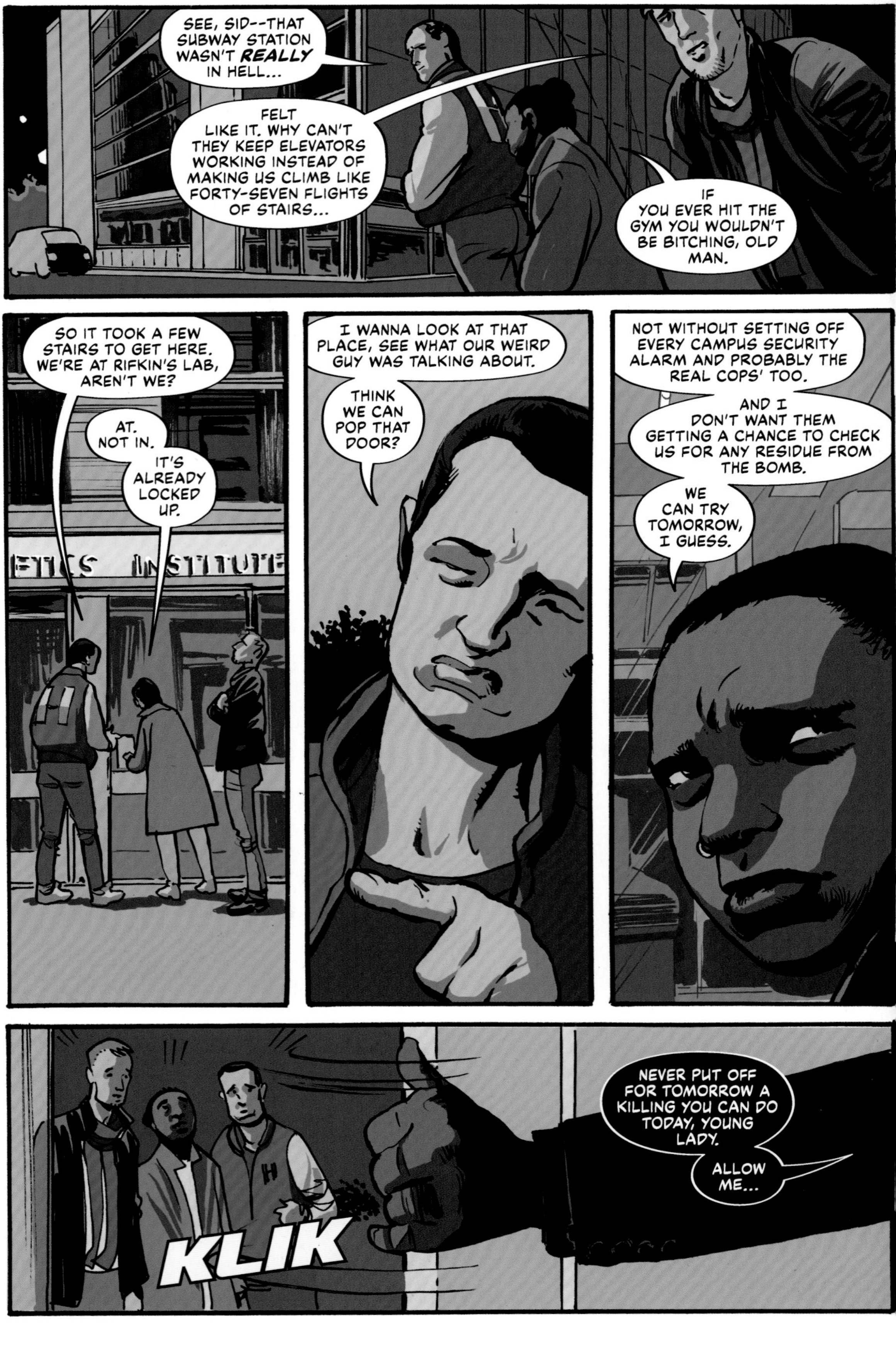

SEE, SID--THAT SUBWAY STATION WASN'T REALLY IN HELL...
FELT LIKE IT. WHY CAN'T THEY KEEP ELEVATORS WORKING INSTEAD OF MAKING US CLIMB LIKE FORTY-SEVEN FLIGHTS OF STAIRS...
IF YOU EVER HIT THE GYM YOU WOULDN'T BE BITCHING, OLD MAN.
SO IT TOOK A FEW STAIRS TO GET HERE. WE'RE AT RIFKIN'S LAB, AREN'T WE?
AT. NOT IN.
IT'S ALREADY LOCKED UP.
ETICS INSTITUTE
I WANNA LOOK AT THAT PLACE, SEE WHAT OUR WEIRD GUY WAS TALKING ABOUT.
THINK WE CAN POP THAT DOOR?
NOT WITHOUT SETTING OFF EVERY CAMPUS SECURITY ALARM AND PROBABLY THE REAL COPS' TOO.
AND I DON'T WANT THEM GETTING A CHANCE TO CHECK US FOR ANY RESIDUE FROM THE BOMB.
WE CAN TRY TOMORROW, I GUESS.
NEVER PUT OFF FOR TOMORROW A KILLING YOU CAN DO TODAY, YOUNG LADY.
ALLOW ME...
KLIK

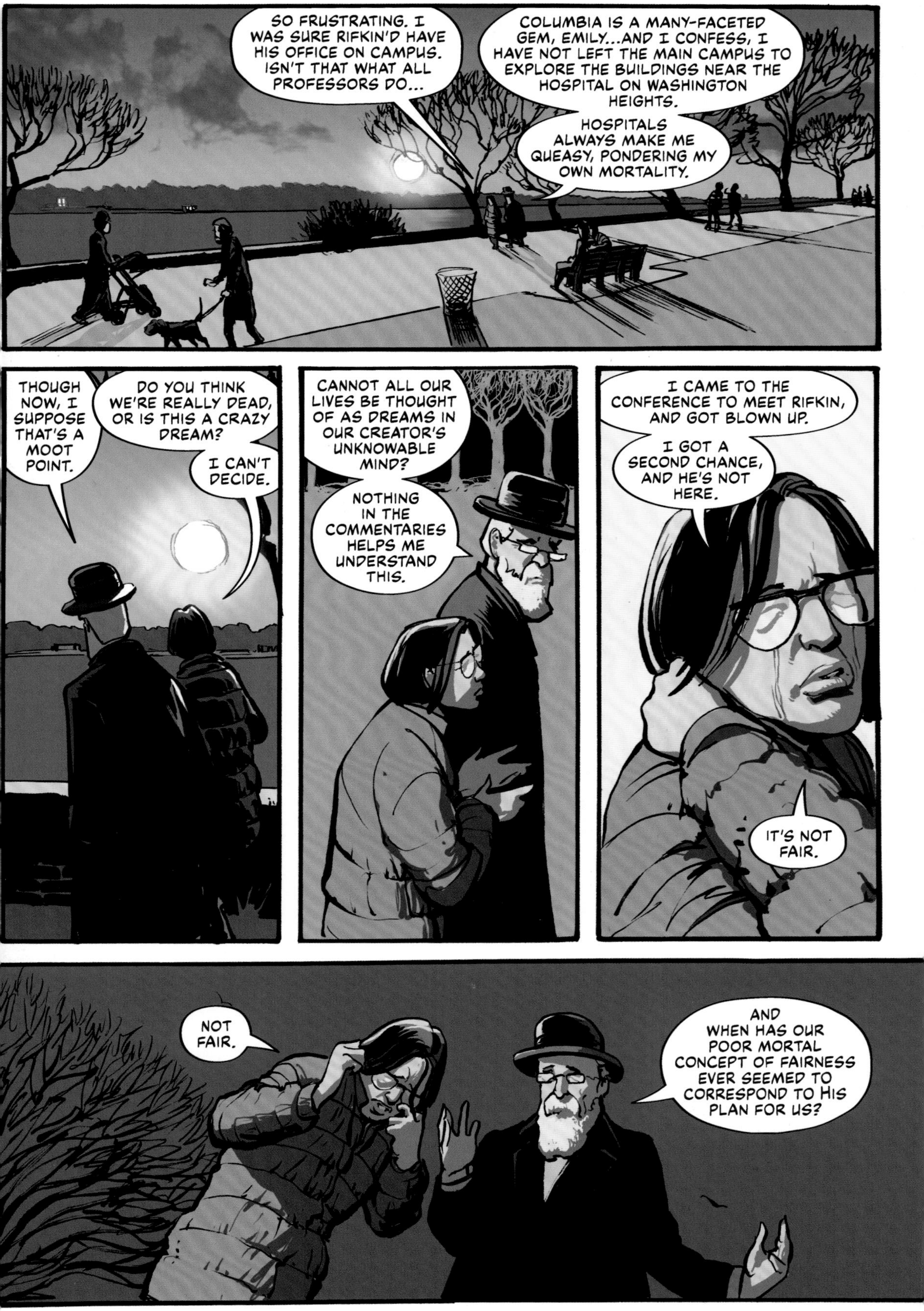
SO FRUSTRATING. I WAS SURE RIFKIN'D HAVE HIS OFFICE ON CAMPUS. ISN'T THAT WHAT ALL PROFESSORS DO...
COLUMBIA IS A MANY-FACETED GEM, EMILY...AND I CONFESS, I HAVE NOT LEFT THE MAIN CAMPUS TO EXPLORE THE BUILDINGS NEAR THE HOSPITAL ON WASHINGTON HEIGHTS.
HOSPITALS ALWAYS MAKE ME QUEASY, PONDERING MY OWN MORTALITY.
THOUGH NOW, I SUPPOSE THAT'S A MOOT POINT.
DO YOU THINK WE'RE REALLY DEAD, OR IS THIS A CRAZY DREAM?
I CAN'T DECIDE.
CANNOT ALL OUR LIVES BE THOUGHT OF AS DREAMS IN OUR CREATOR'S UNKNOWABLE MIND?
NOTHING IN THE COMMENTARIES HELPS ME UNDERSTAND THIS.
I CAME TO THE CONFERENCE TO MEET RIFKIN, AND GOT BLOWN UP.
I GOT A SECOND CHANCE, AND HE'S NOT HERE.
IT'S NOT FAIR.
NOT FAIR.
AND WHEN HAS OUR POOR MORTAL CONCEPT OF FAIRNESS EVER SEEMED TO CORRESPOND TO HIS PLAN FOR US?

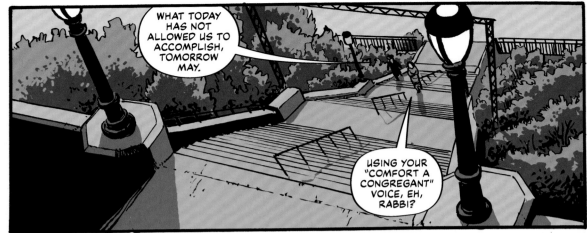

WHAT TODAY HAS NOT ALLOWED US TO ACCOMPLISH, TOMORROW MAY.

USING YOUR "COMFORT A CONGREGANT" VOICE, EH, RABBI?

I LEARNED THAT IN THE SEMINARY TOO.

DON'T TRY IT ON ME.

BESIDES, I JUST THOUGHT OF SOMETHING THAT BARTENDER SAID...

ABOUT HOW HEAVEN CAN WAIT ONE DAY.

WHAT IF WE DON'T *HAVE* TOMORROW?

THERE ARE TIMES WHEN DIVINE INSPIRATION MUST OVERRULE LOGIC, I SUPPOSE.

IF ONLY MY KNEES WOULD AGREE.

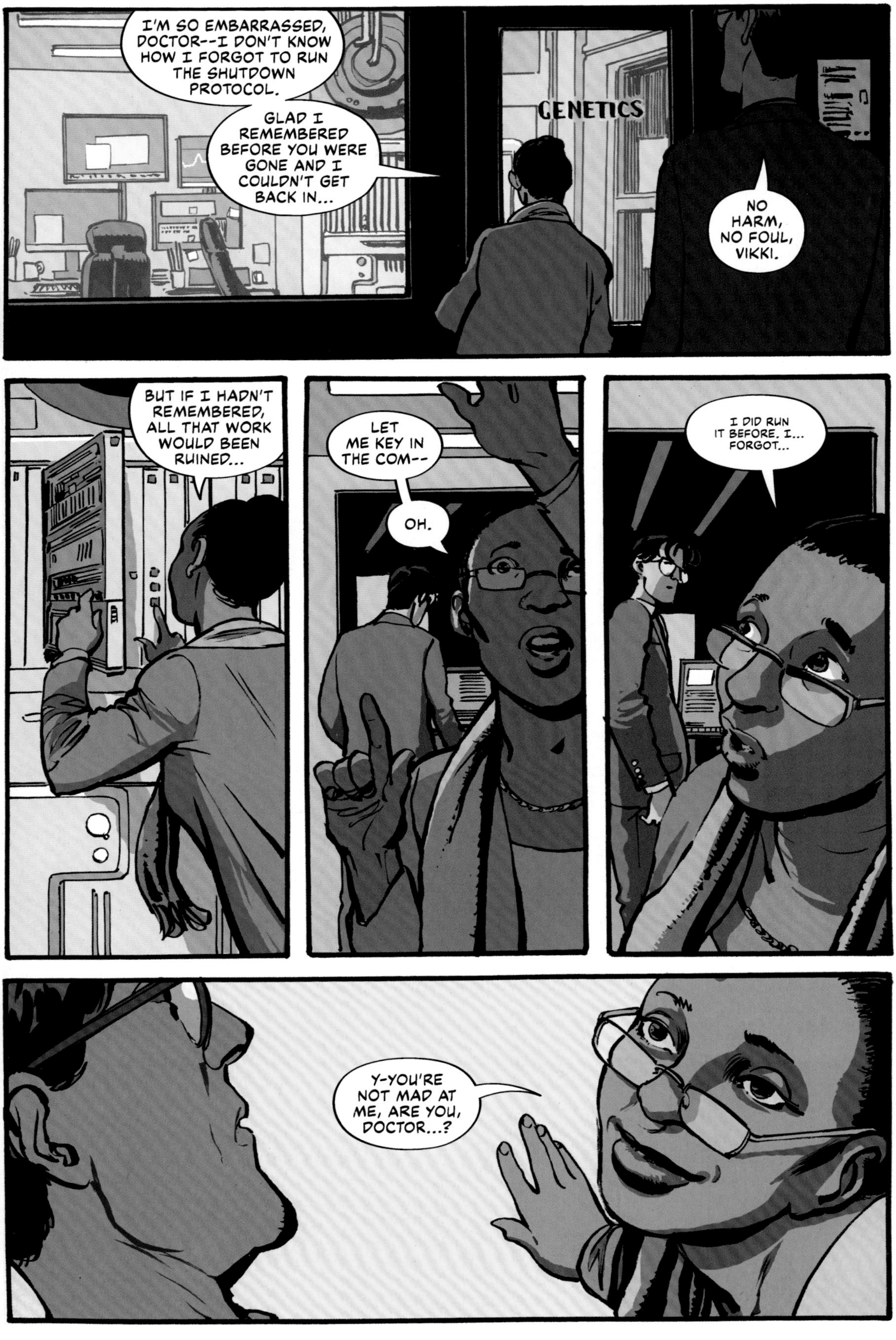
I'M SO EMBARRASSED, DOCTOR--I DON'T KNOW HOW I FORGOT TO RUN THE SHUTDOWN PROTOCOL.
GLAD I REMEMBERED BEFORE YOU WERE GONE AND I COULDN'T GET BACK IN...
GENETICS
NO HARM, NO FOUL, VIKKI.
BUT IF I HADN'T REMEMBERED, ALL THAT WORK WOULD BEEN RUINED...
LET ME KEY IN THE COM--
OH.
I DID RUN IT BEFORE. I... FORGOT...
Y-YOU'RE NOT MAD AT ME, ARE YOU, DOCTOR...?

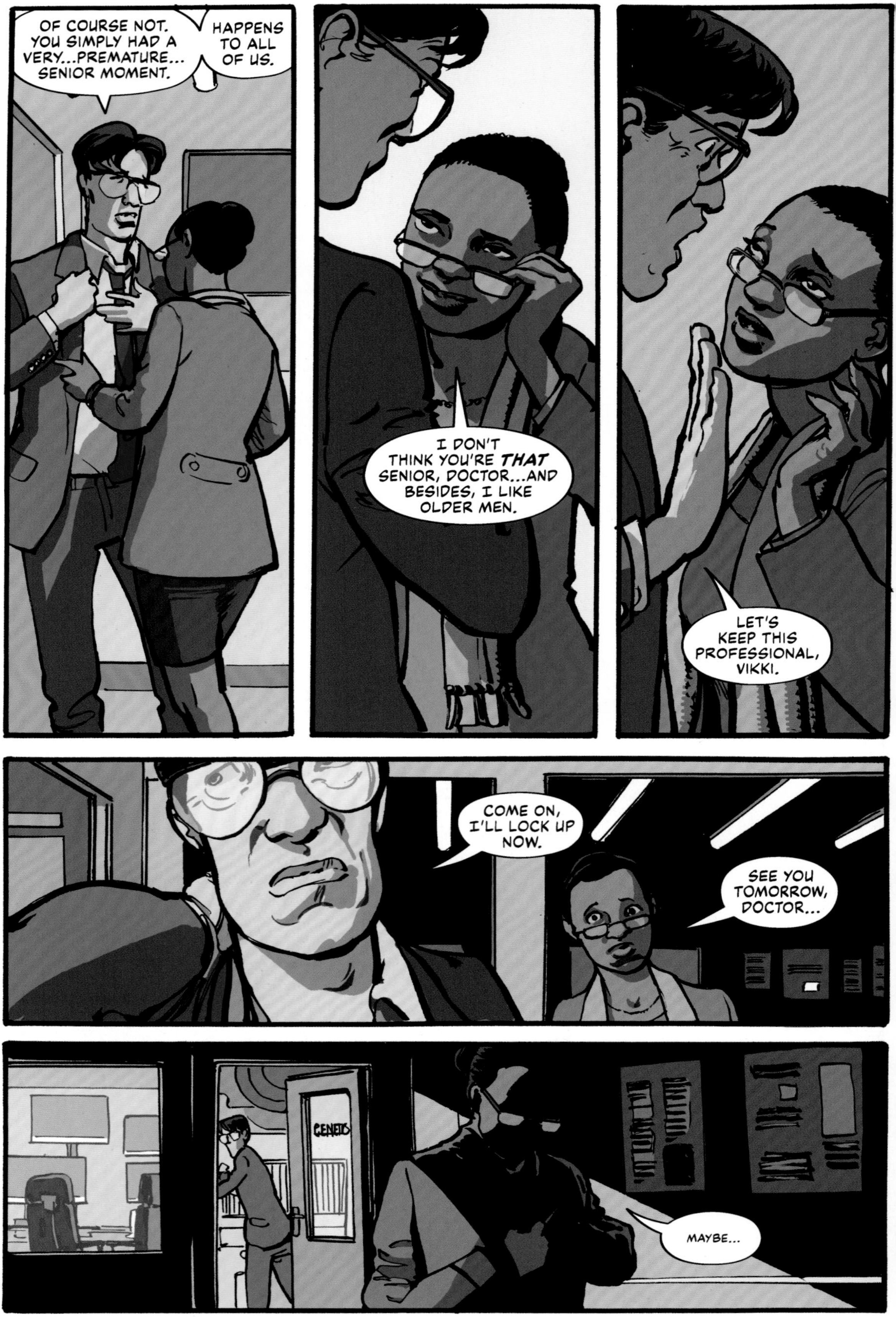
OF COURSE NOT. YOU SIMPLY HAD A VERY...PREMATURE... SENIOR MOMENT.
HAPPENS TO ALL OF US.
I DON'T THINK YOU'RE *THAT* SENIOR, DOCTOR...AND BESIDES, I LIKE OLDER MEN.
LET'S KEEP THIS PROFESSIONAL, VIKKI.
COME ON, I'LL LOCK UP NOW.
SEE YOU TOMORROW, DOCTOR...
GENETICS
MAYBE...

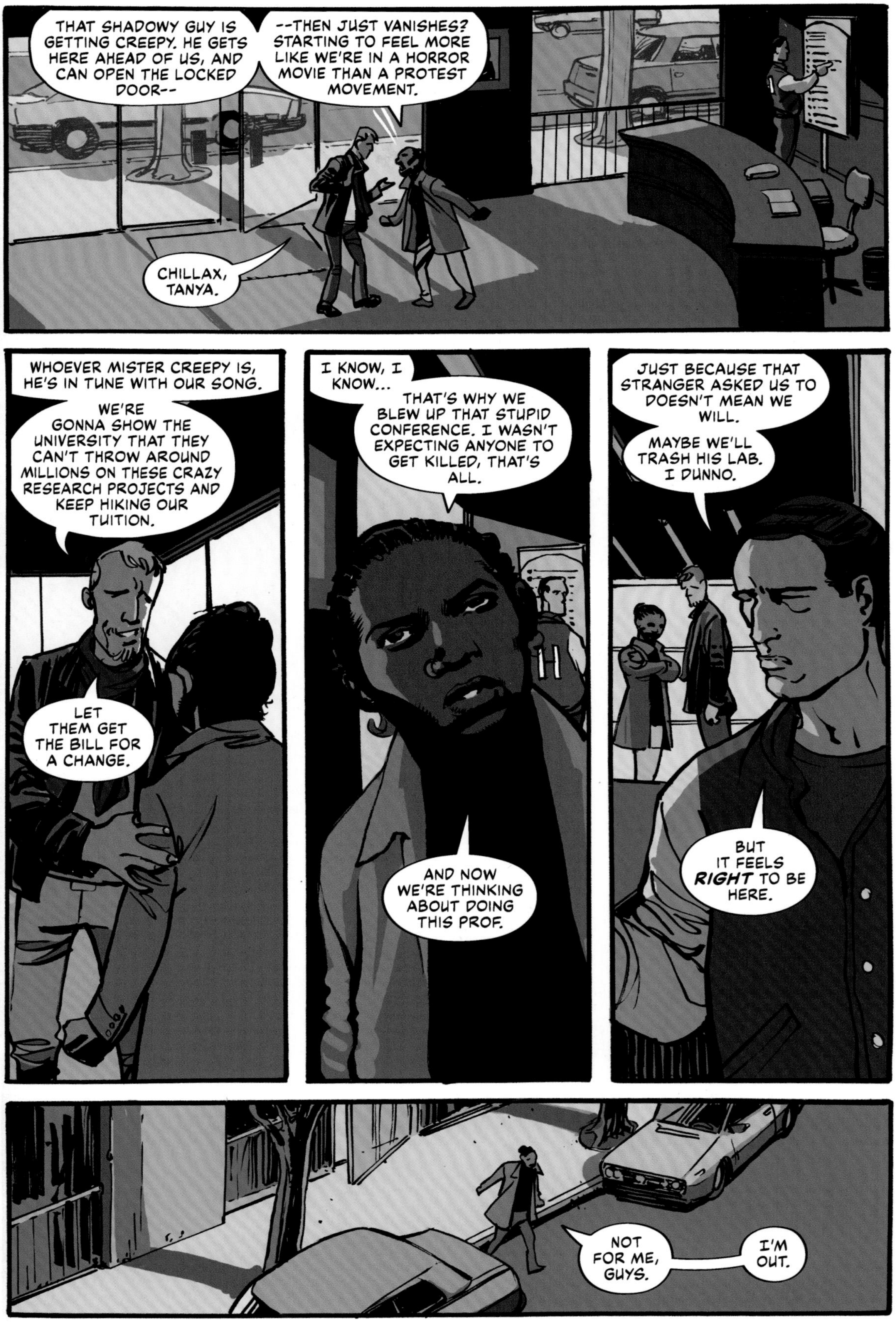
THAT SHADOWY GUY IS GETTING CREEPY. HE GETS HERE AHEAD OF US, AND CAN OPEN THE LOCKED DOOR--
--THEN JUST VANISHES? STARTING TO FEEL MORE LIKE WE'RE IN A HORROR MOVIE THAN A PROTEST MOVEMENT.
CHILLAX, TANYA.
WHOEVER MISTER CREEPY IS, HE'S IN TUNE WITH OUR SONG.
WE'RE GONNA SHOW THE UNIVERSITY THAT THEY CAN'T THROW AROUND MILLIONS ON THESE CRAZY RESEARCH PROJECTS AND KEEP HIKING OUR TUITION.
LET THEM GET THE BILL FOR A CHANGE.
I KNOW, I KNOW...
THAT'S WHY WE BLEW UP THAT STUPID CONFERENCE. I WASN'T EXPECTING ANYONE TO GET KILLED, THAT'S ALL.
AND NOW WE'RE THINKING ABOUT DOING THIS PROF.
JUST BECAUSE THAT STRANGER ASKED US TO DOESN'T MEAN WE WILL.
MAYBE WE'LL TRASH HIS LAB. I DUNNO.
BUT IT FEELS *RIGHT* TO BE HERE.
NOT FOR ME, GUYS.
I'M OUT.

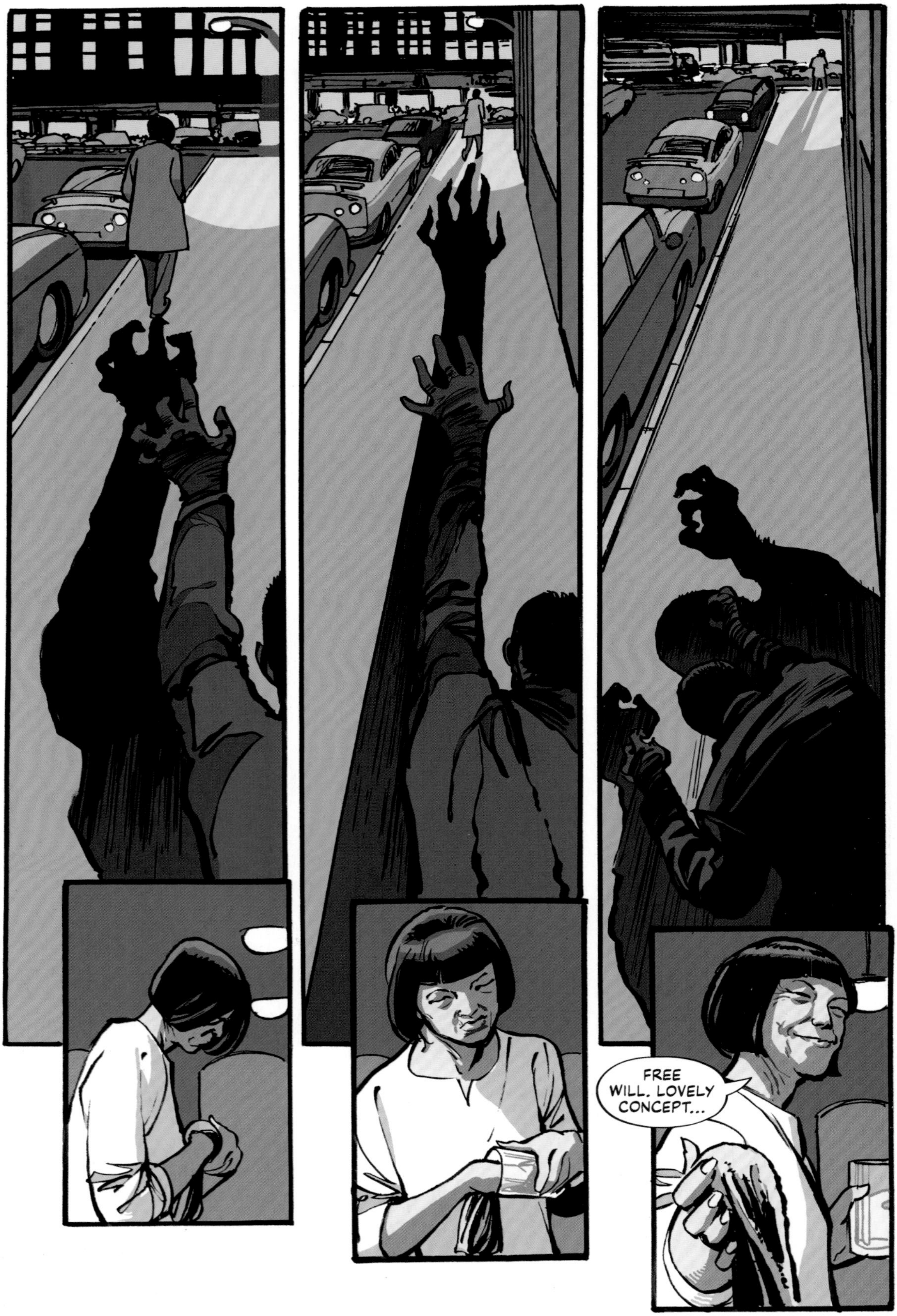
FREE WILL. LOVELY CONCEPT...

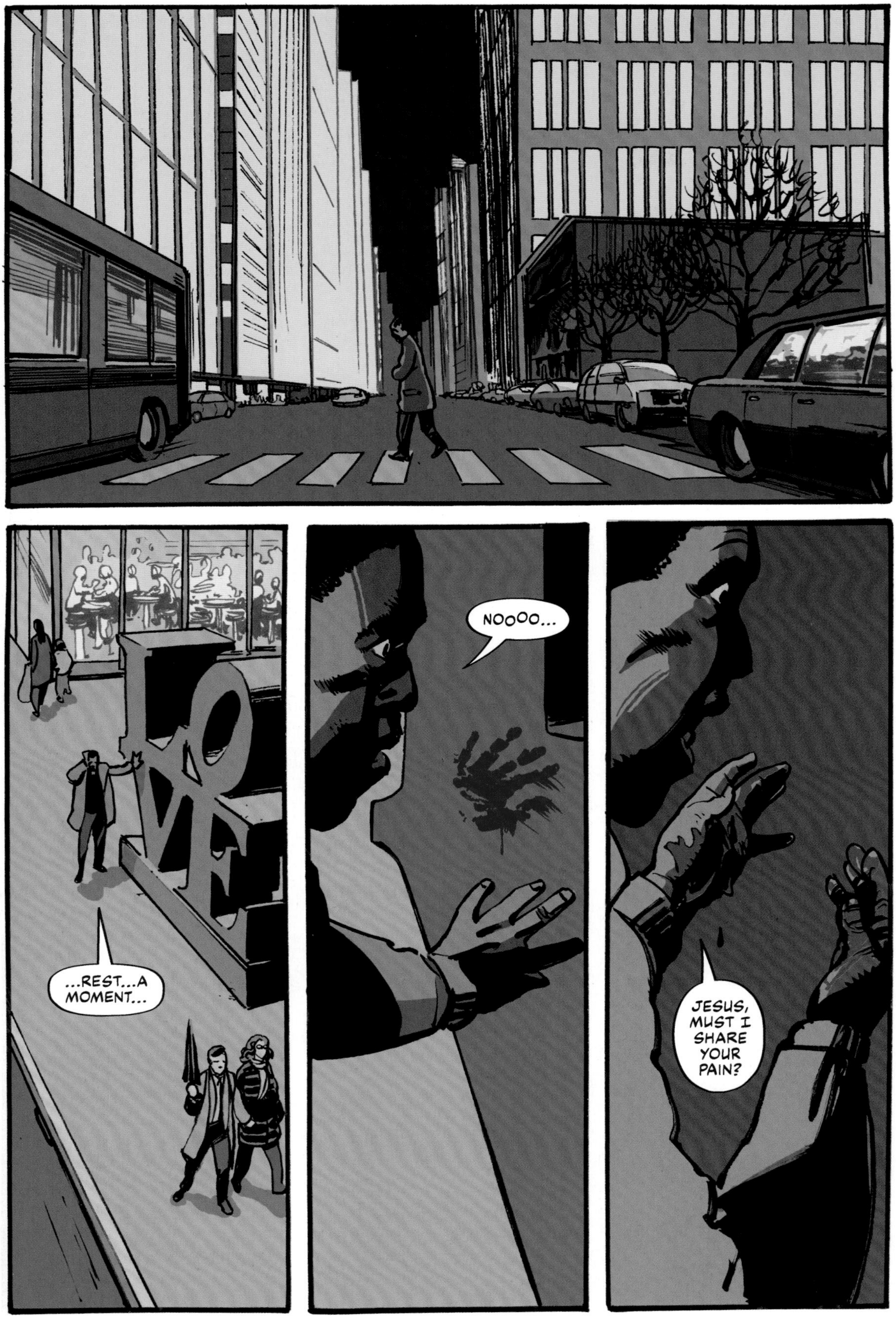
...REST...A MOMENT...
NOOOO...
JESUS, MUST I SHARE YOUR PAIN?

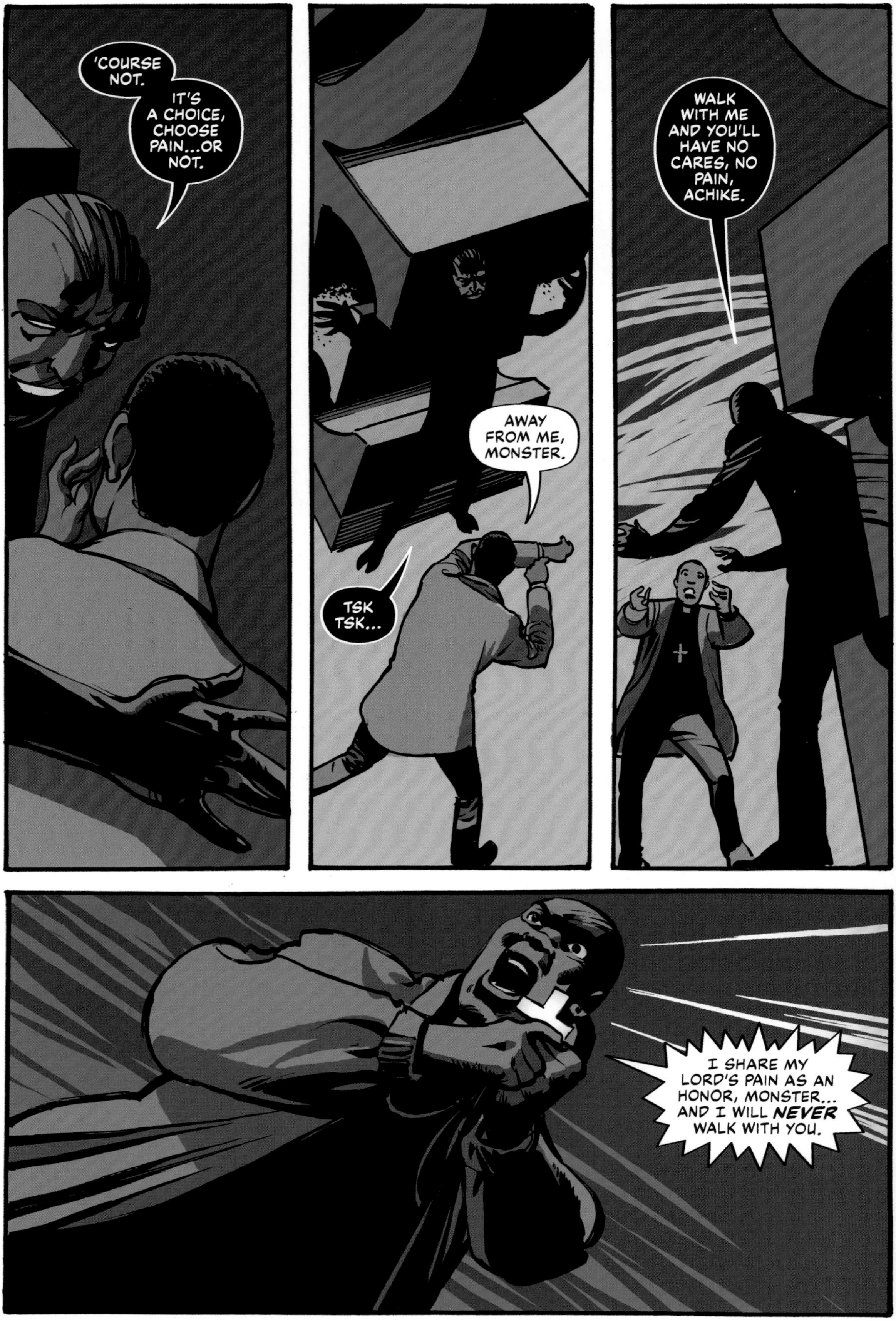
'COURSE NOT.
IT'S A CHOICE, CHOOSE PAIN...OR NOT.
AWAY FROM ME, MONSTER.
TSK TSK...
WALK WITH ME AND YOU'LL HAVE NO CARES, NO PAIN, ACHIKE.
I SHARE MY LORD'S PAIN AS AN HONOR, MONSTER... AND I WILL *NEVER* WALK WITH YOU.

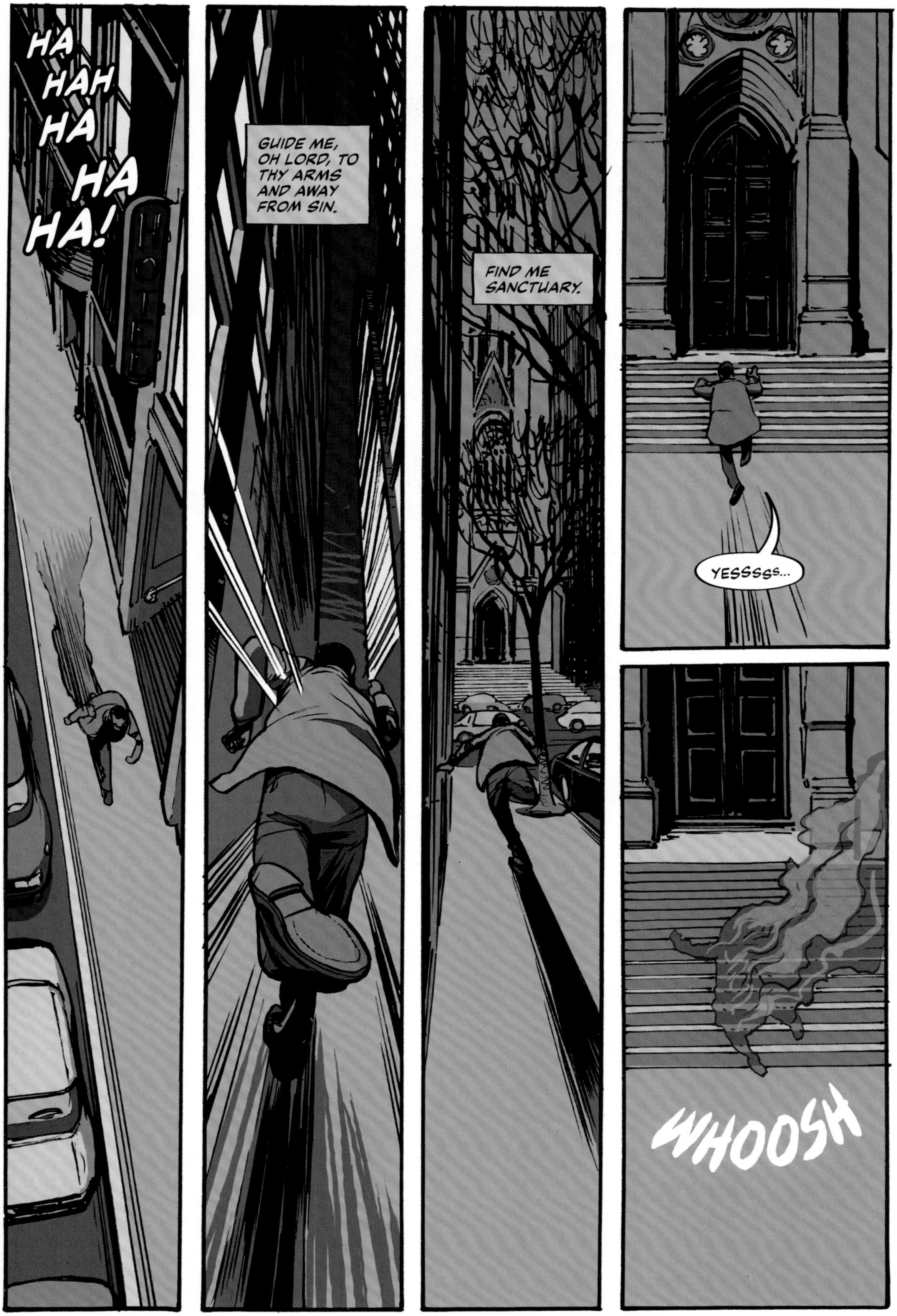
HA HAH HA HA HA!
GUIDE ME, OH LORD, TO THY ARMS AND AWAY FROM SIN.
FIND ME SANCTUARY.
YESSSSS...
WHOOSH

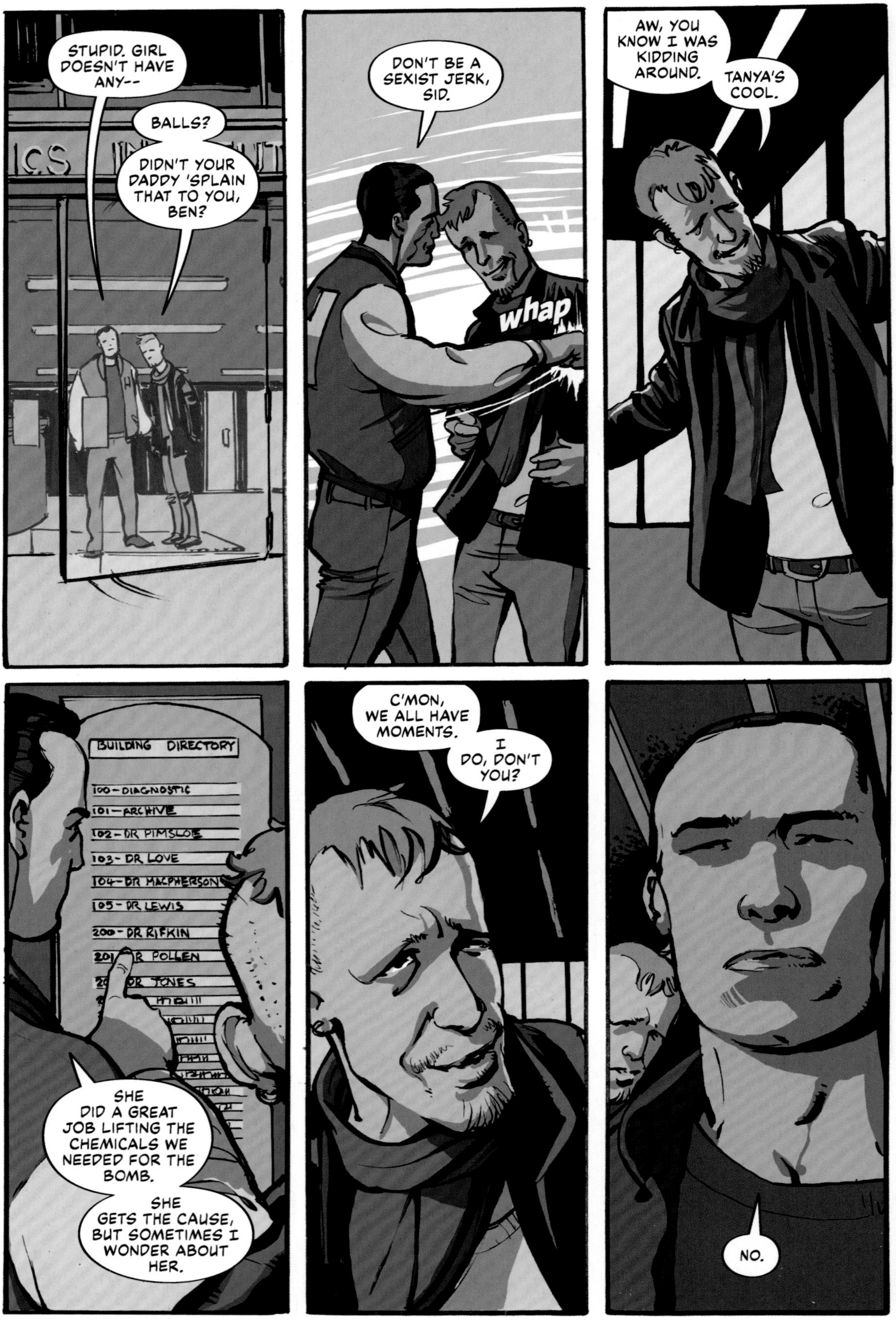
STUPID. GIRL DOESN'T HAVE ANY--
BALLS?
DIDN'T YOUR DADDY 'SPLAIN THAT TO YOU, BEN?
DON'T BE A SEXIST JERK, SID.
whap
AW, YOU KNOW I WAS KIDDING AROUND.
TANYA'S COOL.
BUILDING DIRECTORY
100-DIAGNOSTIC
101-ARCHIVE
102-DR PIMSLOE
103-DR LOVE
104-DR MACPHERSON
105-DR LEWIS
200-DR RIFKIN
SHE DID A GREAT JOB LIFTING THE CHEMICALS WE NEEDED FOR THE BOMB.
SHE GETS THE CAUSE, BUT SOMETIMES I WONDER ABOUT HER.
C'MON, WE ALL HAVE MOMENTS.
I DO, DON'T YOU?
NO.

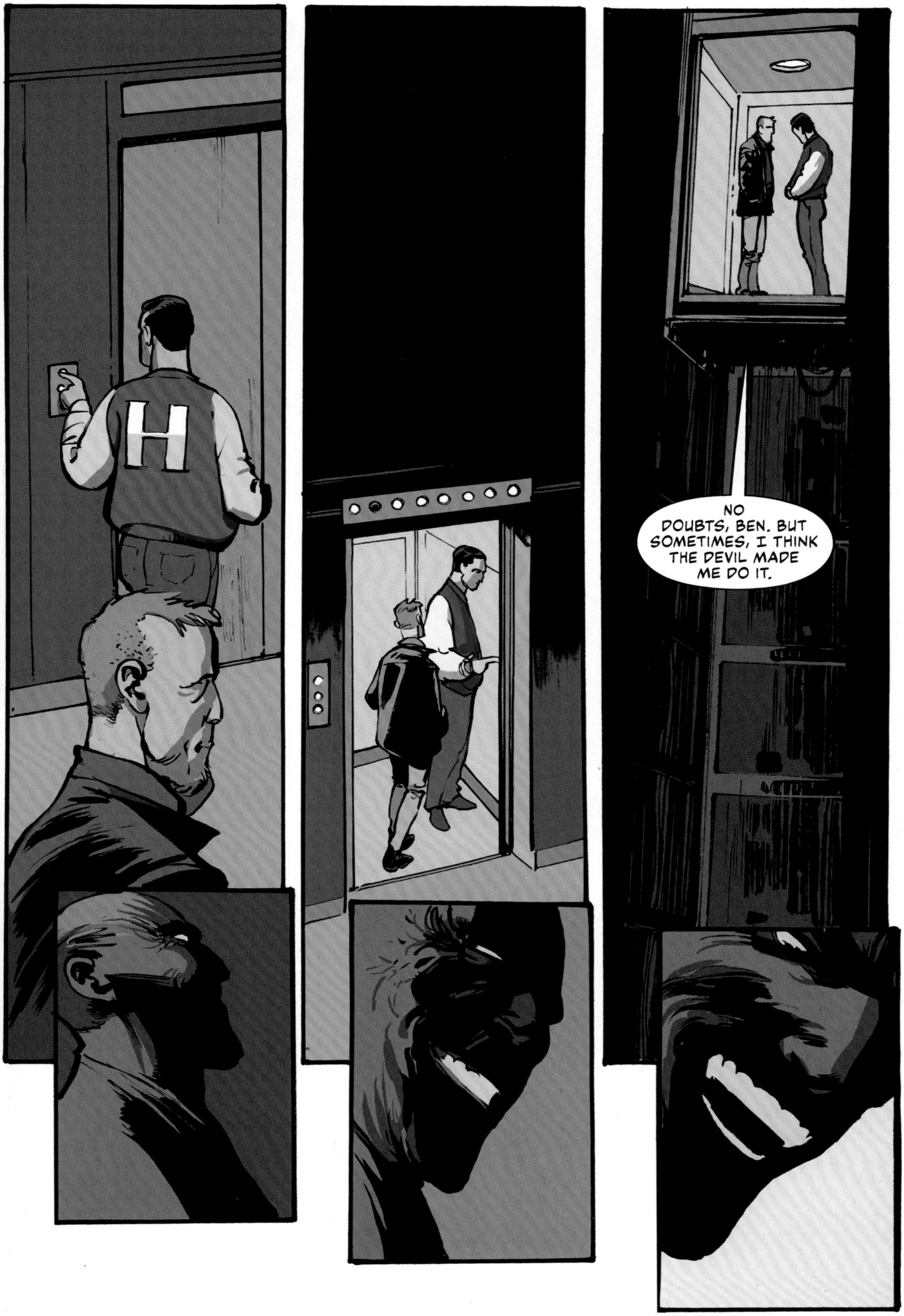
NO DOUBTS, BEN. BUT SOMETIMES, I THINK THE DEVIL MADE ME DO IT.

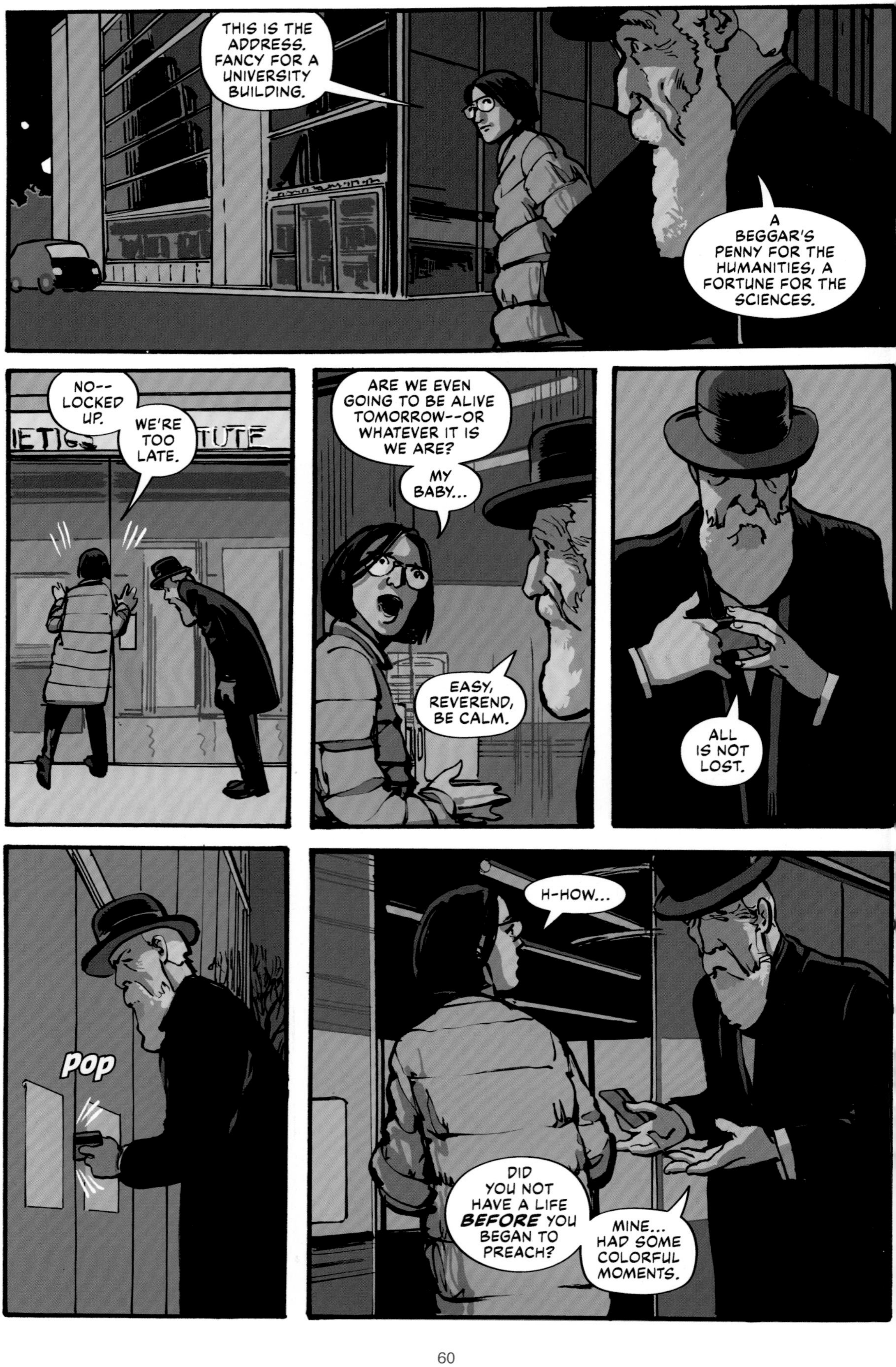
THIS IS THE ADDRESS. FANCY FOR A UNIVERSITY BUILDING.
A BEGGAR'S PENNY FOR THE HUMANITIES, A FORTUNE FOR THE SCIENCES.
NO-- LOCKED UP.
WE'RE TOO LATE.
ARE WE EVEN GOING TO BE ALIVE TOMORROW--OR WHATEVER IT IS WE ARE?
MY BABY...
EASY, REVEREND, BE CALM.
ALL IS NOT LOST.
pop
H-HOW...
DID YOU NOT HAVE A LIFE ***BEFORE*** YOU BEGAN TO PREACH?
MINE... HAD SOME COLORFUL MOMENTS.

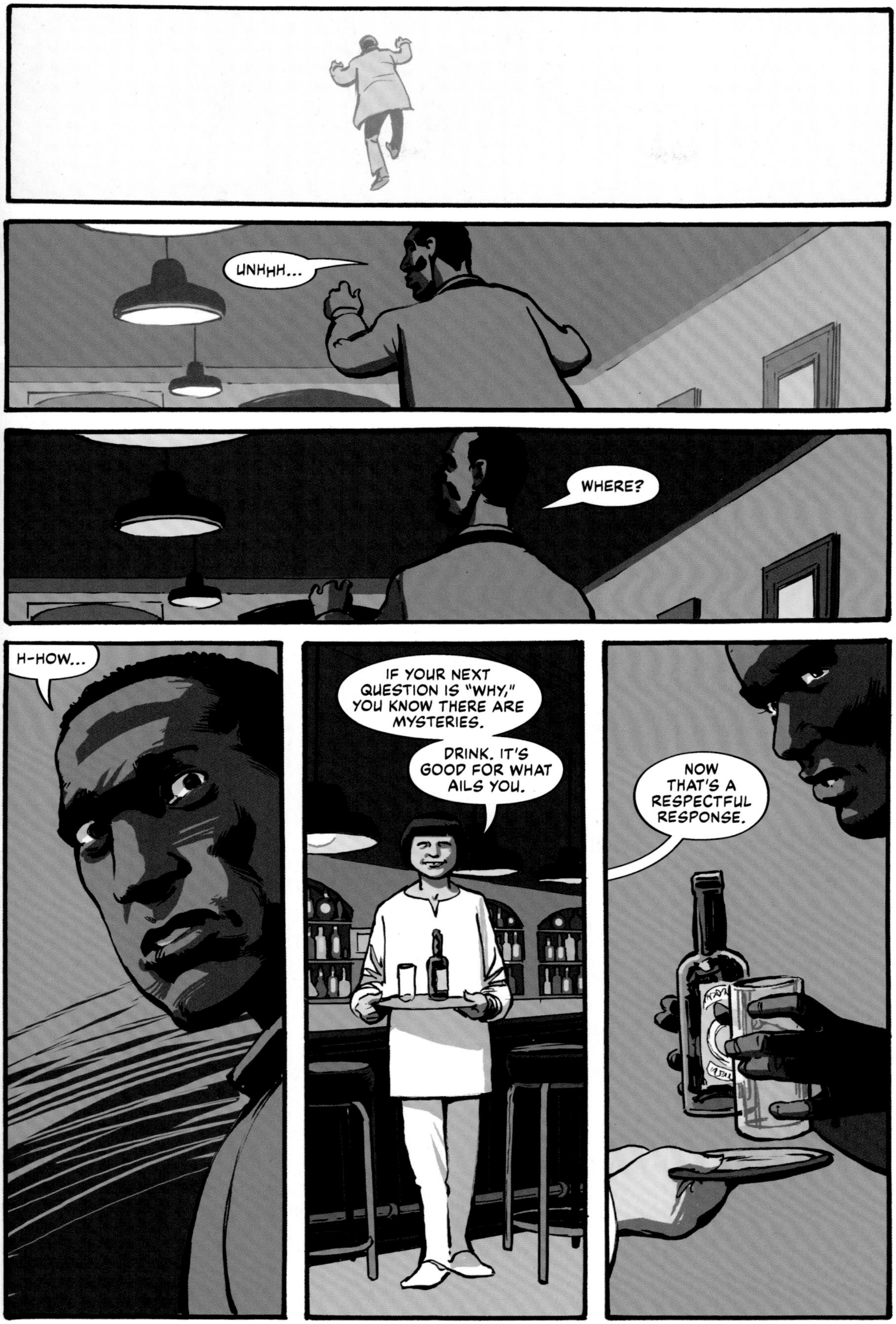
UNHHH...
WHERE?
H-HOW...
IF YOUR NEXT QUESTION IS "WHY," YOU KNOW THERE ARE MYSTERIES.
DRINK. IT'S GOOD FOR WHAT AILS YOU.
NOW THAT'S A RESPECTFUL RESPONSE.

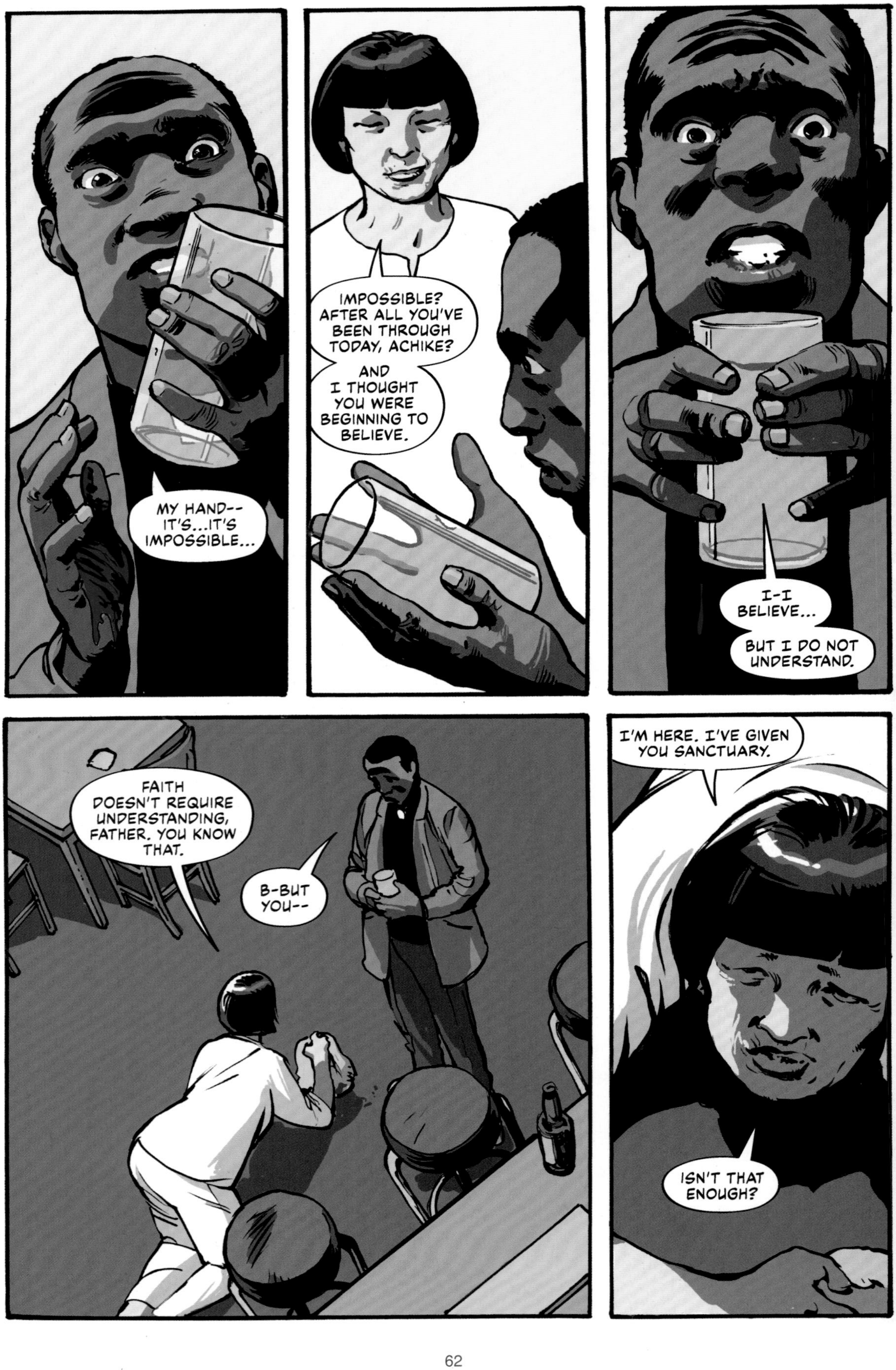

MY HAND-- IT'S...IT'S IMPOSSIBLE...
IMPOSSIBLE? AFTER ALL YOU'VE BEEN THROUGH TODAY, ACHIKE?
AND I THOUGHT YOU WERE BEGINNING TO BELIEVE.
I-I BELIEVE...
BUT I DO NOT UNDERSTAND.
FAITH DOESN'T REQUIRE UNDERSTANDING, FATHER. YOU KNOW THAT.
B-BUT YOU--
I'M HERE. I'VE GIVEN YOU SANCTUARY.
ISN'T THAT ENOUGH?

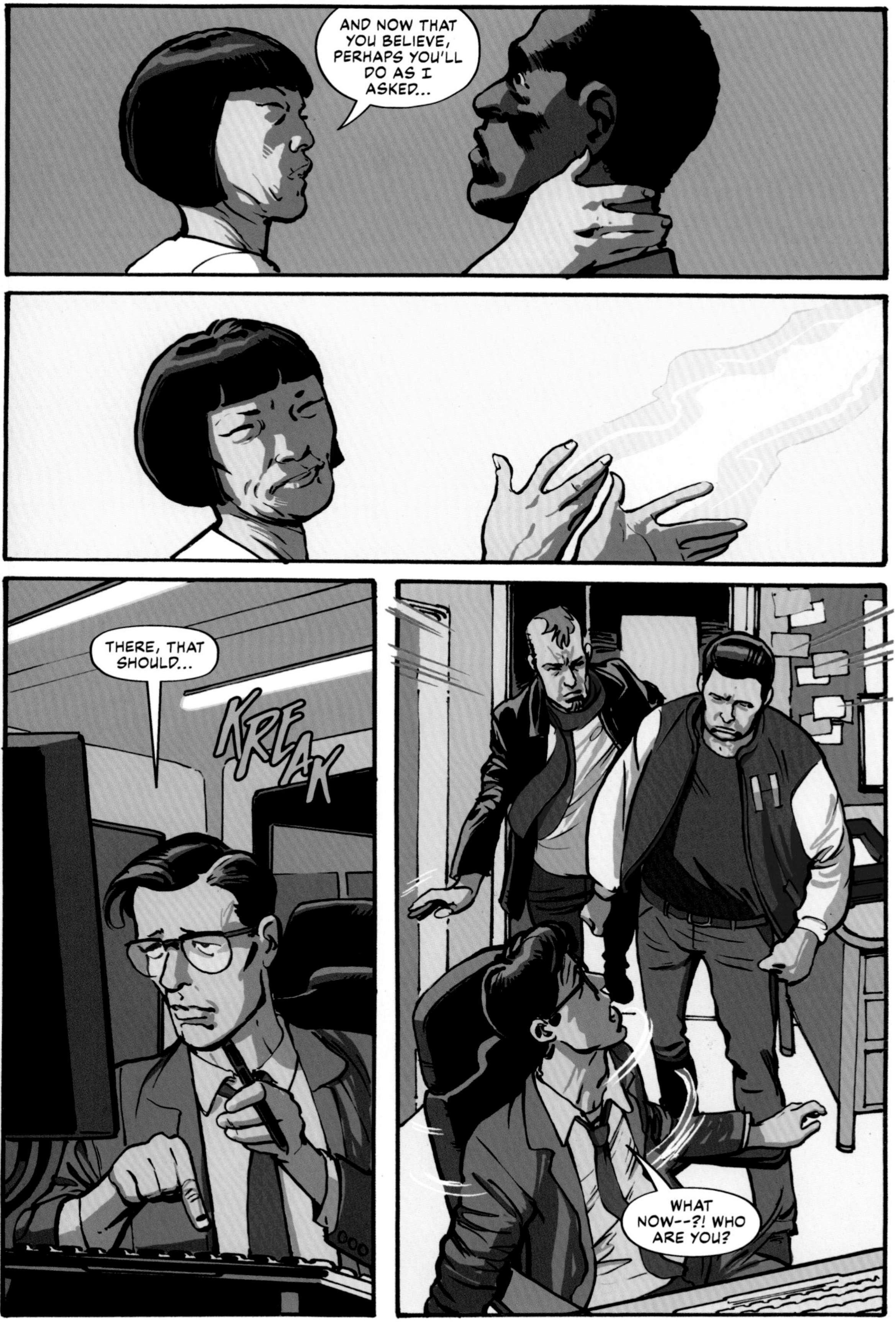
AND NOW THAT YOU BELIEVE, PERHAPS YOU'LL DO AS I ASKED...
THERE, THAT SHOULD...
KREAK
WHAT NOW--?! WHO ARE YOU?

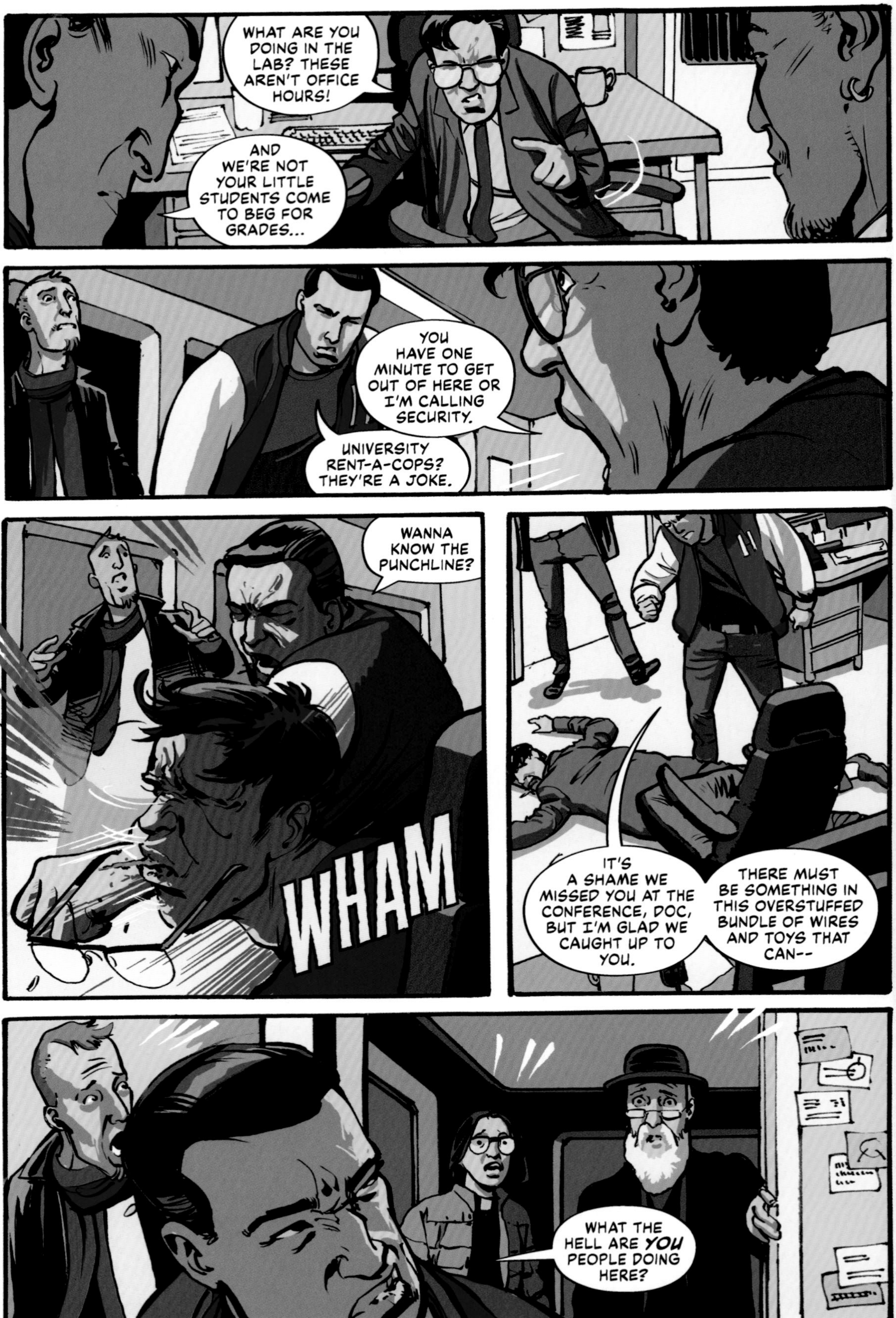
WHAT ARE YOU DOING IN THE LAB? THESE AREN'T OFFICE HOURS!
AND WE'RE NOT YOUR LITTLE STUDENTS COME TO BEG FOR GRADES...
YOU HAVE ONE MINUTE TO GET OUT OF HERE OR I'M CALLING SECURITY.
UNIVERSITY RENT-A-COPS? THEY'RE A JOKE.
WANNA KNOW THE PUNCHLINE?
WHAM
IT'S A SHAME WE MISSED YOU AT THE CONFERENCE, DOC, BUT I'M GLAD WE CAUGHT UP TO YOU.
THERE MUST BE SOMETHING IN THIS OVERSTUFFED BUNDLE OF WIRES AND TOYS THAT CAN--
WHAT THE HELL ARE *YOU* PEOPLE DOING HERE?

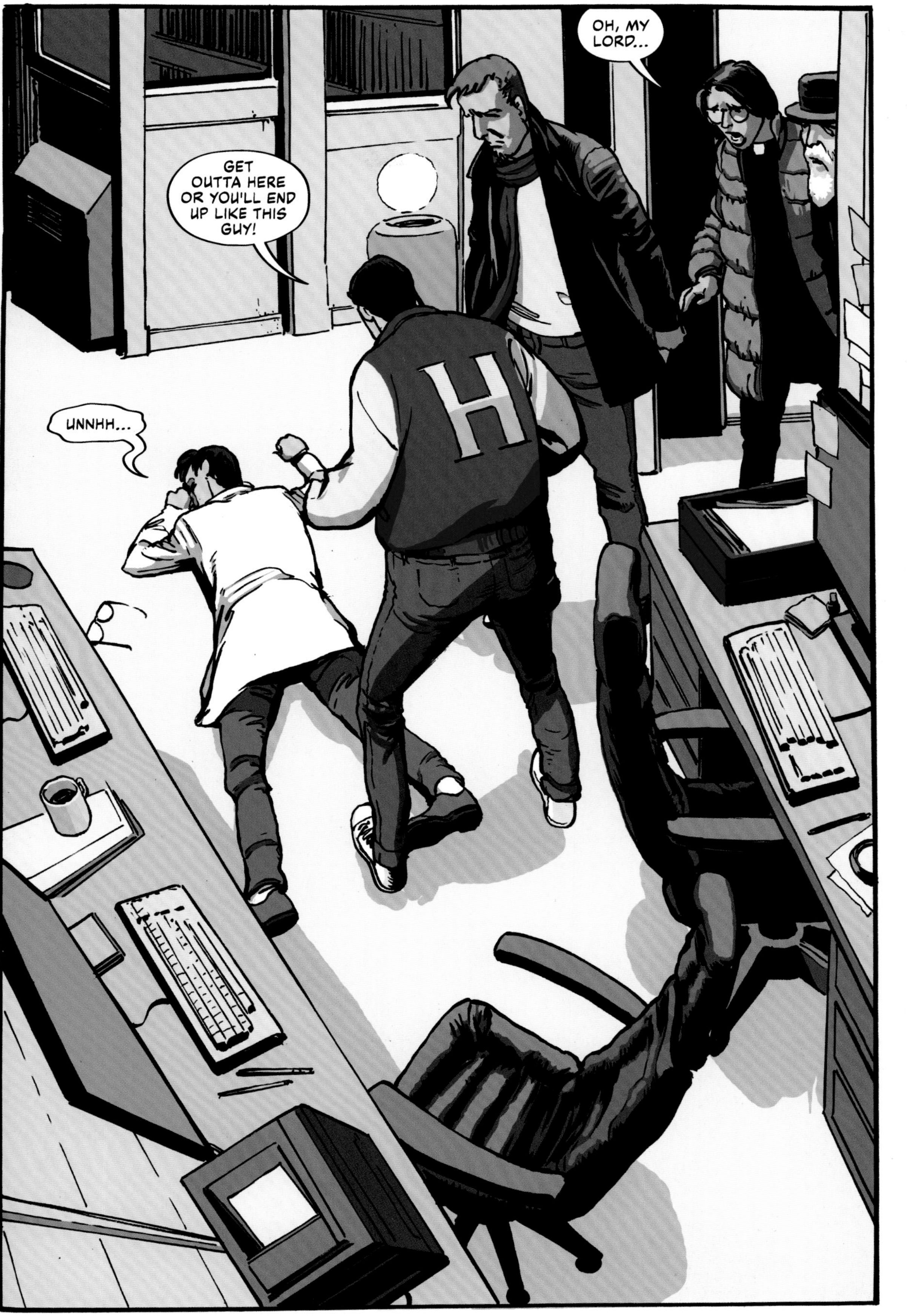
OH, MY LORD...
GET OUTTA HERE OR YOU'LL END UP LIKE THIS GUY!
UNNHH...

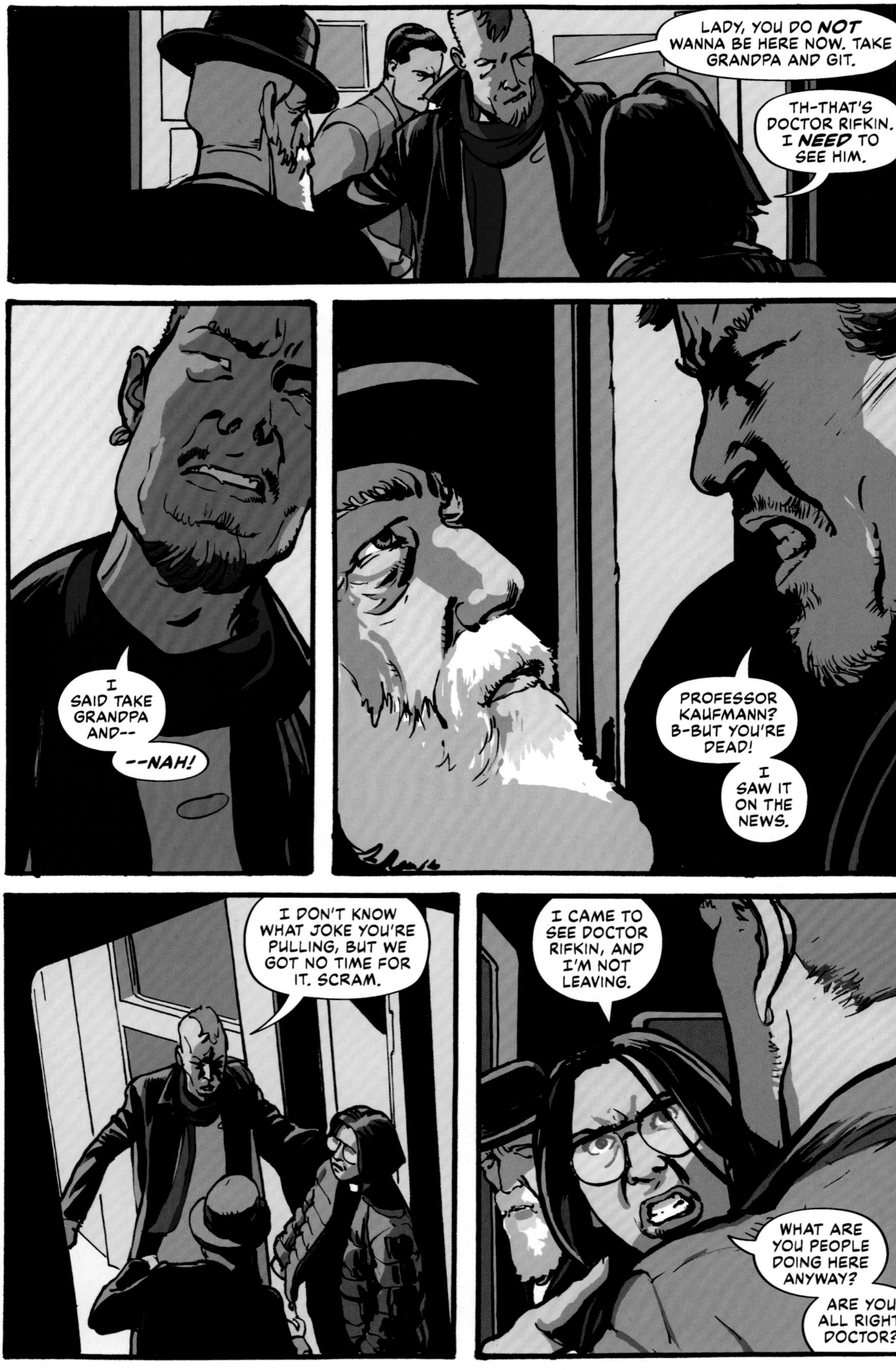
LADY, YOU DO NOT WANNA BE HERE NOW. TAKE GRANDPA AND GIT.
TH-THAT'S DOCTOR RIFKIN. I NEED TO SEE HIM.
I SAID TAKE GRANDPA AND--
--NAH!
PROFESSOR KAUFMANN? B-BUT YOU'RE DEAD!
I SAW IT ON THE NEWS.
I DON'T KNOW WHAT JOKE YOU'RE PULLING, BUT WE GOT NO TIME FOR IT. SCRAM.
I CAME TO SEE DOCTOR RIFKIN, AND I'M NOT LEAVING.
WHAT ARE YOU PEOPLE DOING HERE ANYWAY?
ARE YOU ALL RIGHT, DOCTOR?

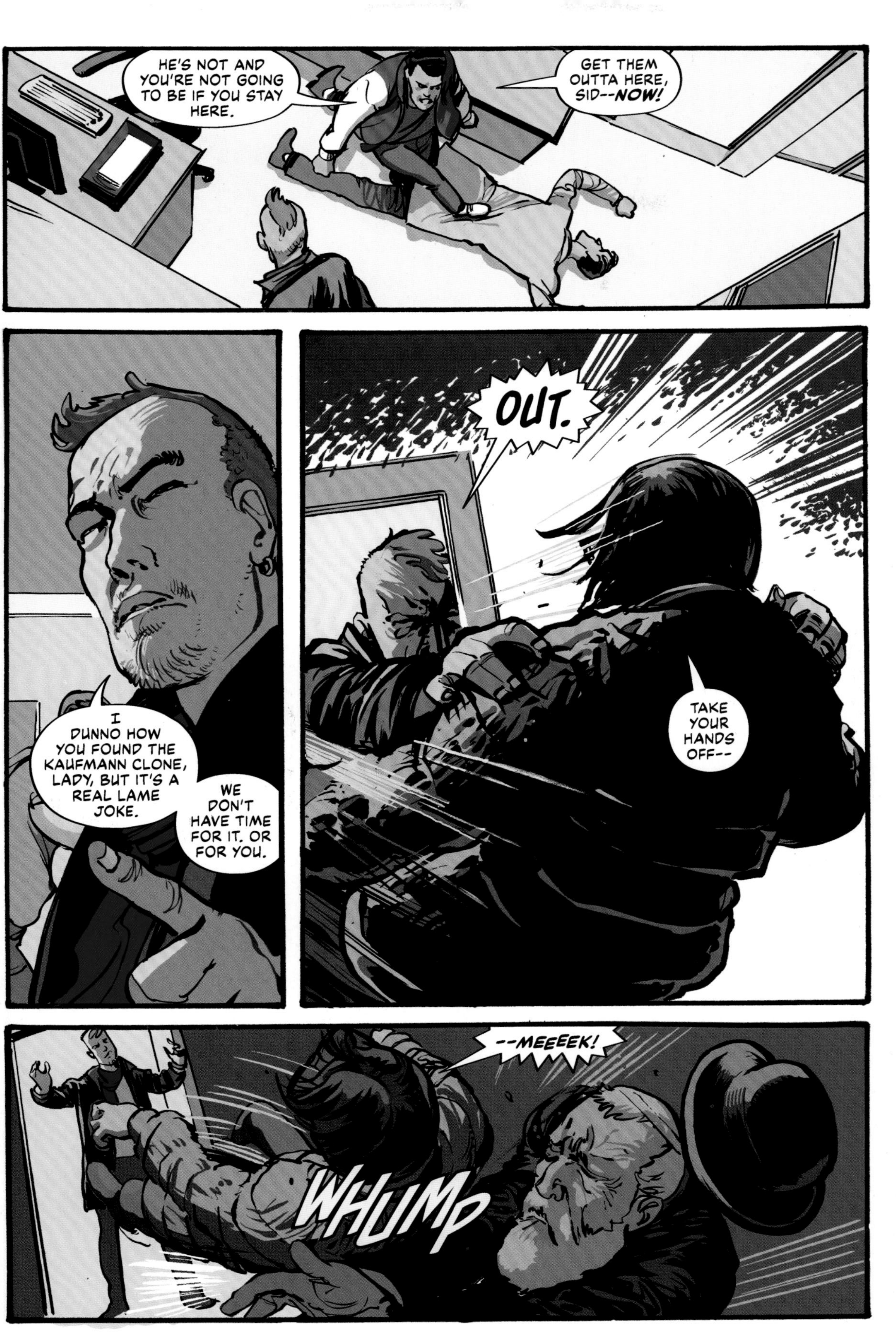
HE'S NOT AND YOU'RE NOT GOING TO BE IF YOU STAY HERE.
GET THEM OUTTA HERE, SID--**NOW!**
I DUNNO HOW YOU FOUND THE KAUFMANN CLONE, LADY, BUT IT'S A REAL LAME JOKE.
WE DON'T HAVE TIME FOR IT. OR FOR YOU.
OUT.
TAKE YOUR HANDS OFF--
--MEEEEK!
WHUMP

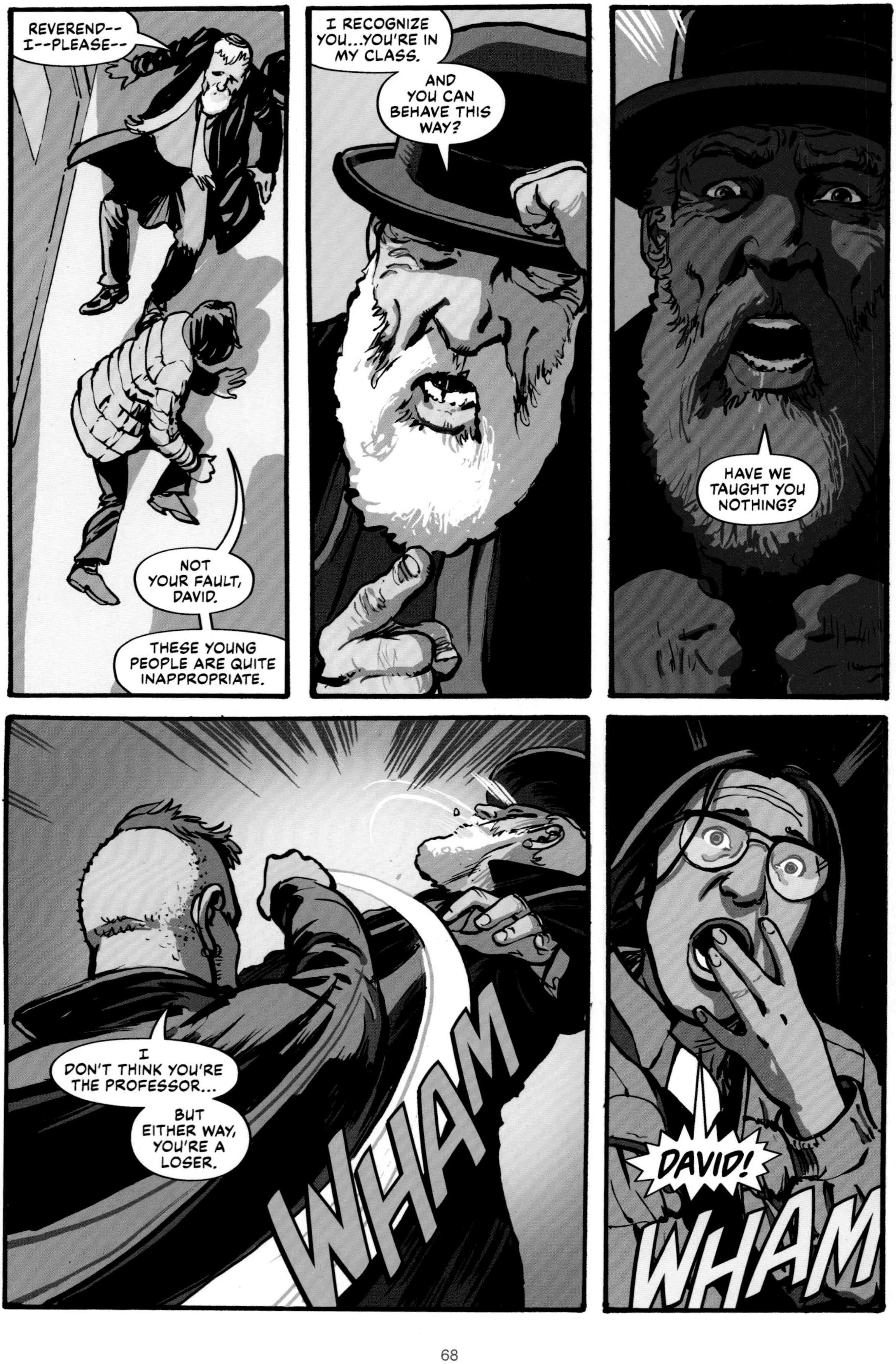

REVEREND-- I--PLEASE--
NOT YOUR FAULT, DAVID.
THESE YOUNG PEOPLE ARE QUITE INAPPROPRIATE.
I RECOGNIZE YOU...YOU'RE IN MY CLASS.
AND YOU CAN BEHAVE THIS WAY?
HAVE WE TAUGHT YOU NOTHING?
I DON'T THINK YOU'RE THE PROFESSOR...
BUT EITHER WAY, YOU'RE A LOSER.
WHAM
DAVID!
WHAM

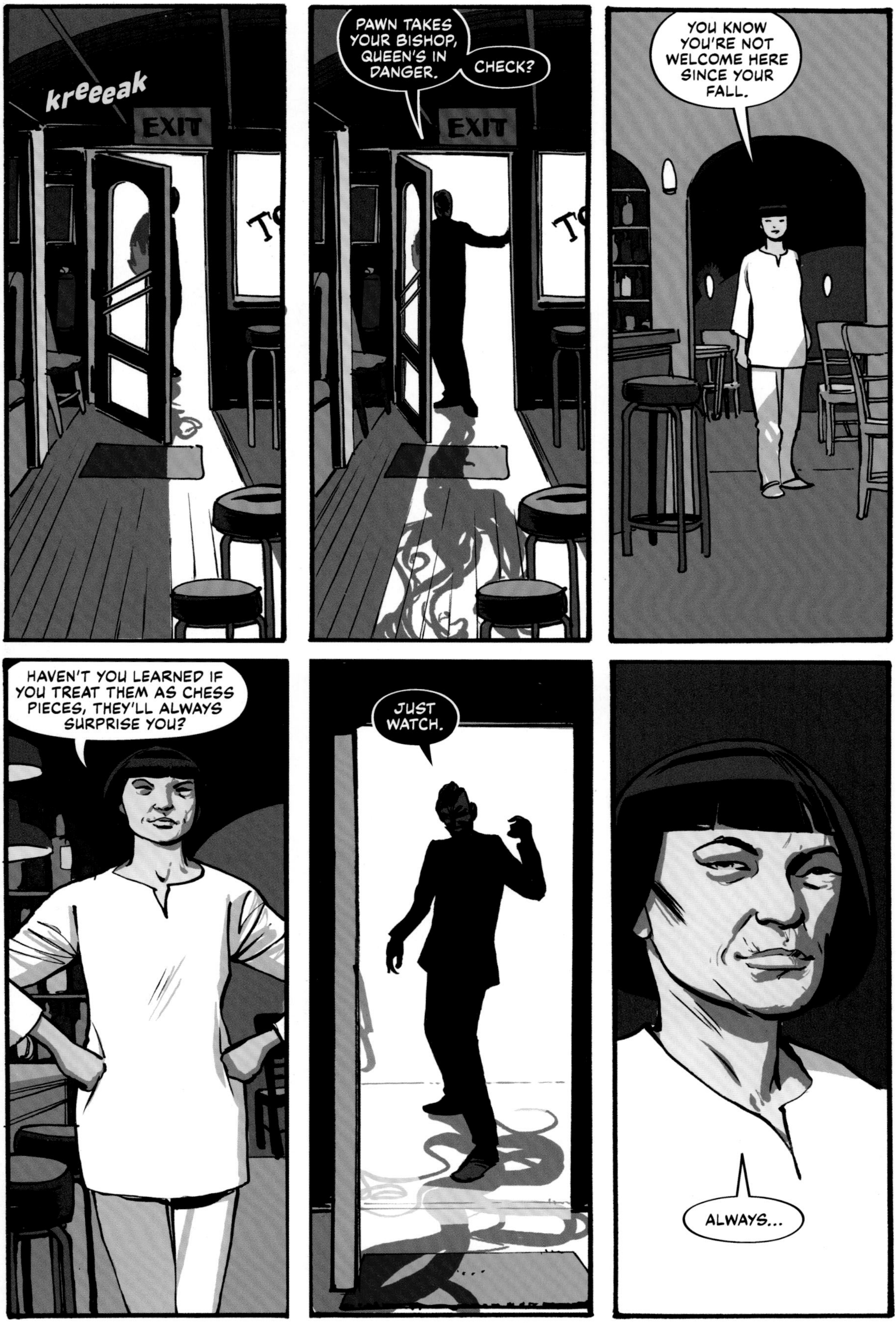
kreeeak
EXIT
PAWN TAKES YOUR BISHOP, QUEEN'S IN DANGER.
CHECK?
EXIT
YOU KNOW YOU'RE NOT WELCOME HERE SINCE YOUR FALL.
HAVEN'T YOU LEARNED IF YOU TREAT THEM AS CHESS PIECES, THEY'LL ALWAYS SURPRISE YOU?
JUST WATCH.
ALWAYS...

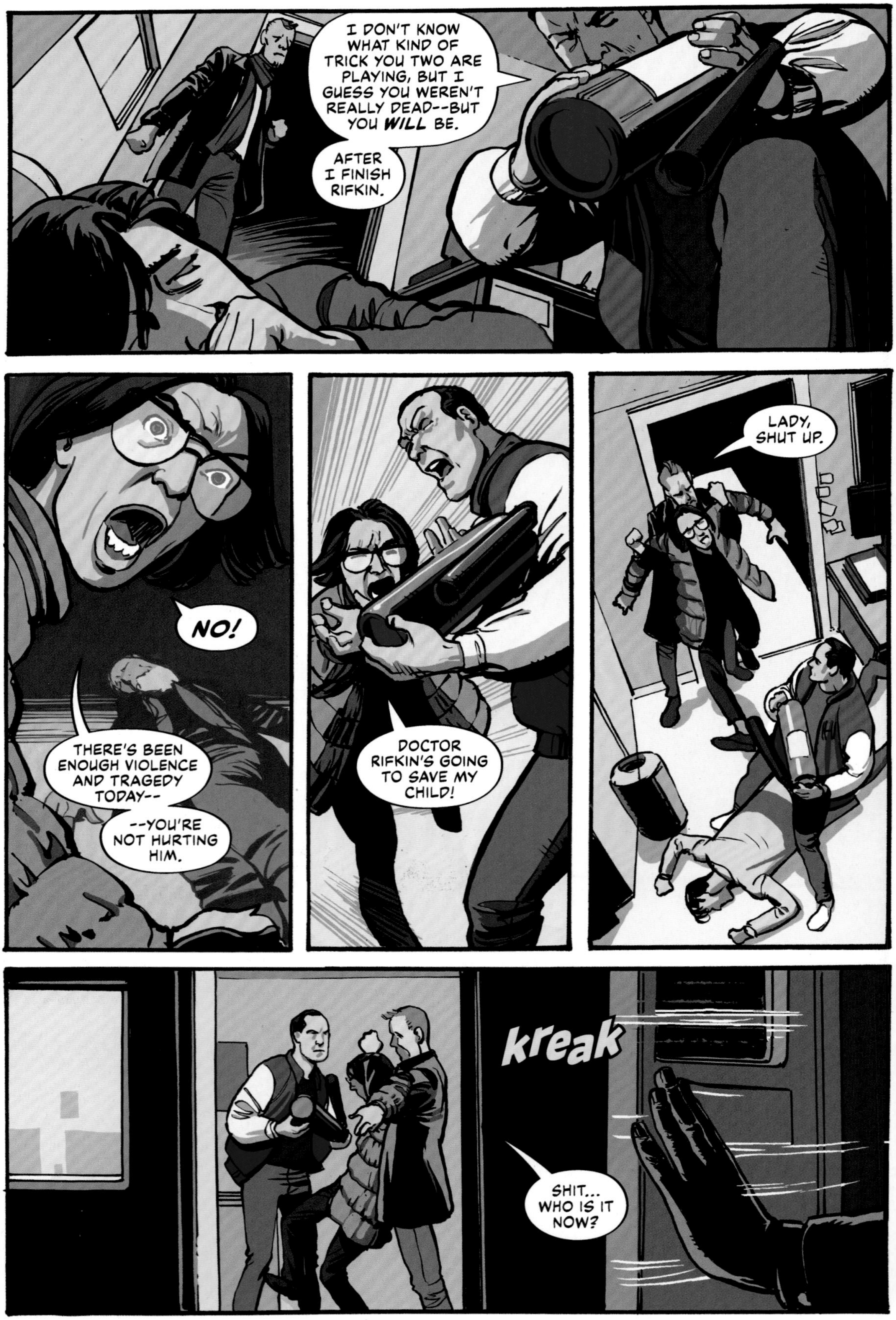
I DON'T KNOW WHAT KIND OF TRICK YOU TWO ARE PLAYING, BUT I GUESS YOU WEREN'T REALLY DEAD--BUT YOU WILL BE.
AFTER I FINISH RIFKIN.
NO!
THERE'S BEEN ENOUGH VIOLENCE AND TRAGEDY TODAY--
--YOU'RE NOT HURTING HIM.
DOCTOR RIFKIN'S GOING TO SAVE MY CHILD!
LADY, SHUT UP.
kreak
SHIT... WHO IS IT NOW?

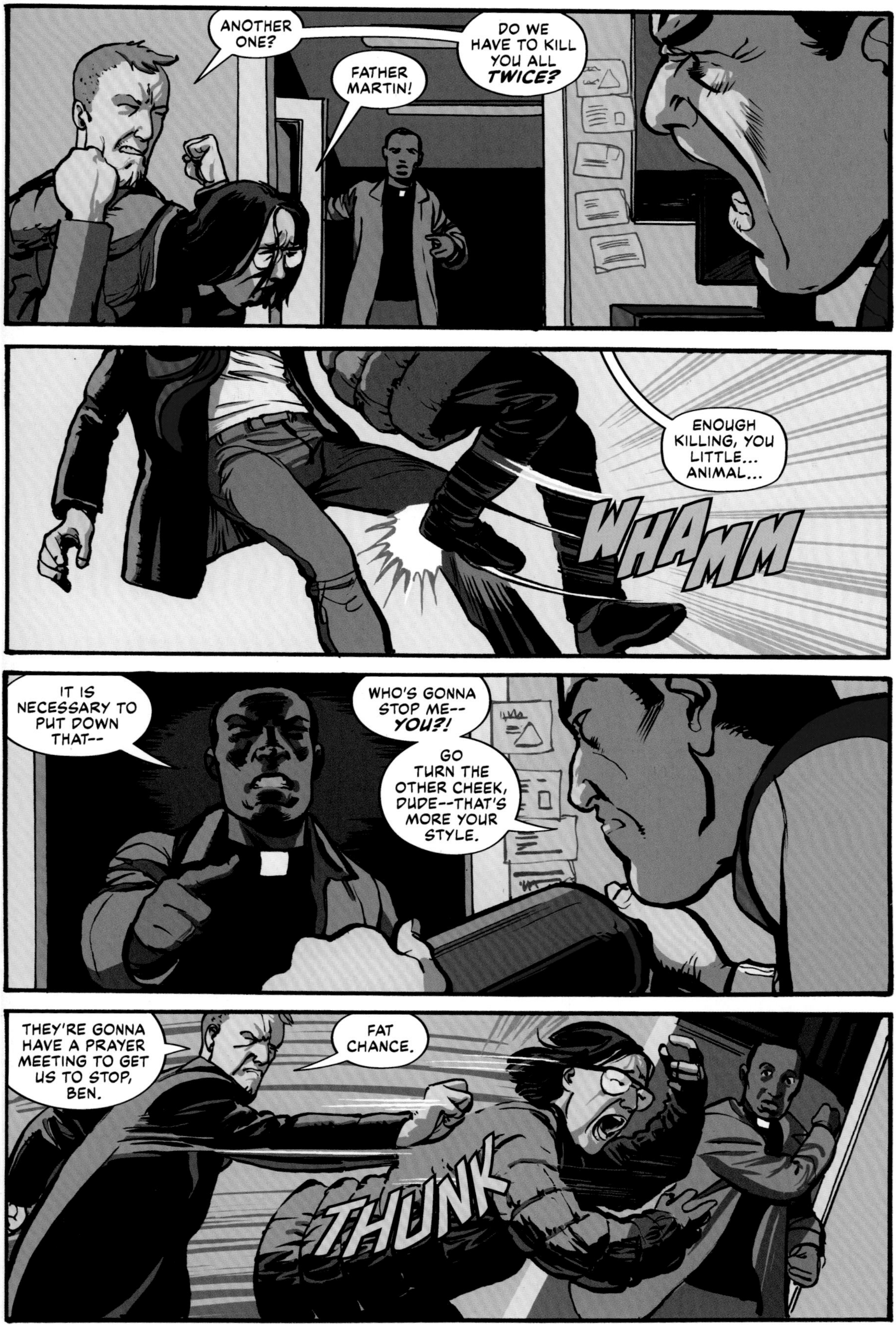
ANOTHER ONE?
DO WE HAVE TO KILL YOU ALL TWICE?
FATHER MARTIN!
ENOUGH KILLING, YOU LITTLE... ANIMAL...
WHAMM
IT IS NECESSARY TO PUT DOWN THAT--
WHO'S GONNA STOP ME-- YOU?!
GO TURN THE OTHER CHEEK, DUDE--THAT'S MORE YOUR STYLE.
THEY'RE GONNA HAVE A PRAYER MEETING TO GET US TO STOP, BEN.
FAT CHANCE.
THUNK

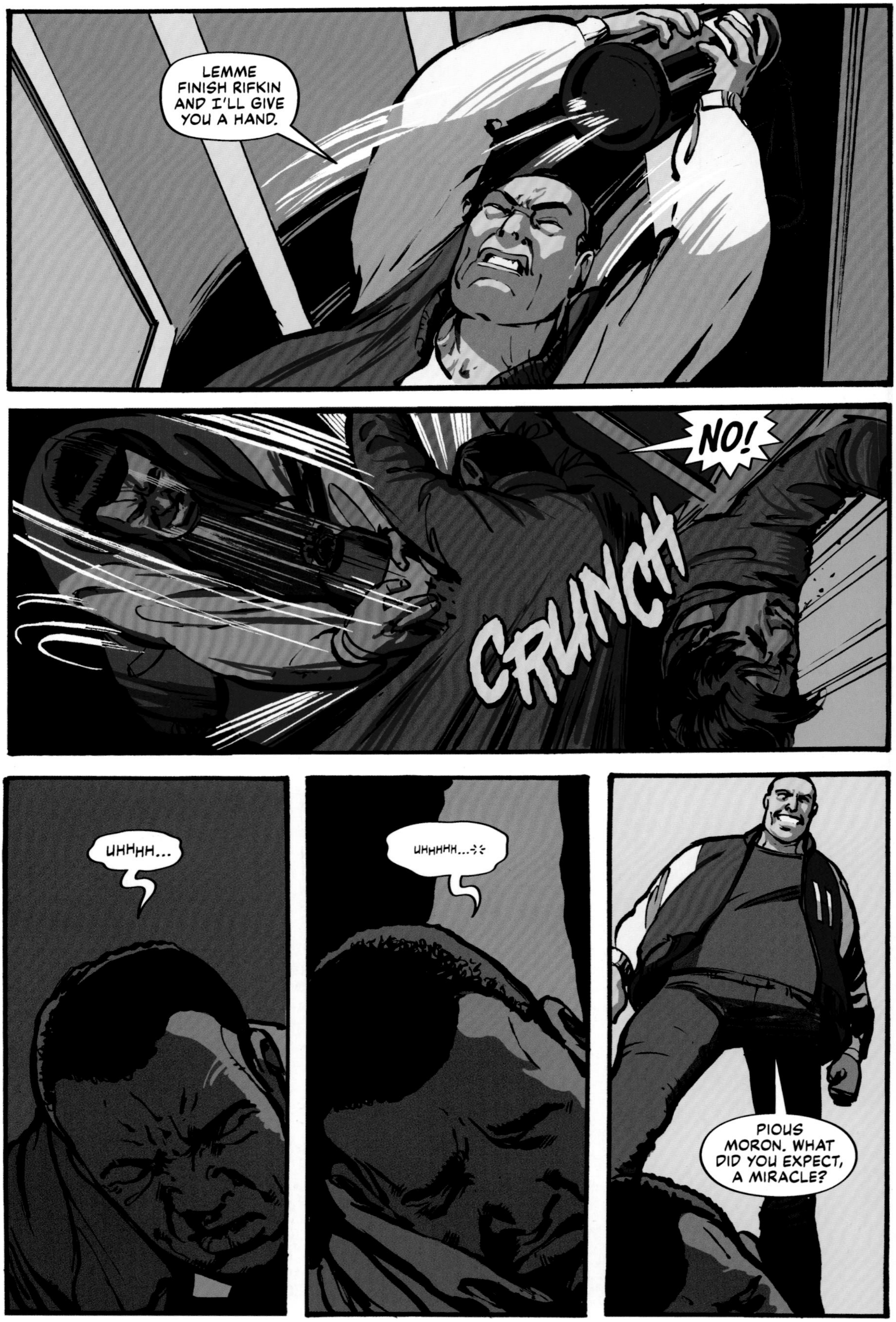
LEMME FINISH RIFKIN AND I'LL GIVE YOU A HAND.
NO!
CRUNCH
UHHHH...
UHHHHH...
PIOUS MORON. WHAT DID YOU EXPECT, A MIRACLE?

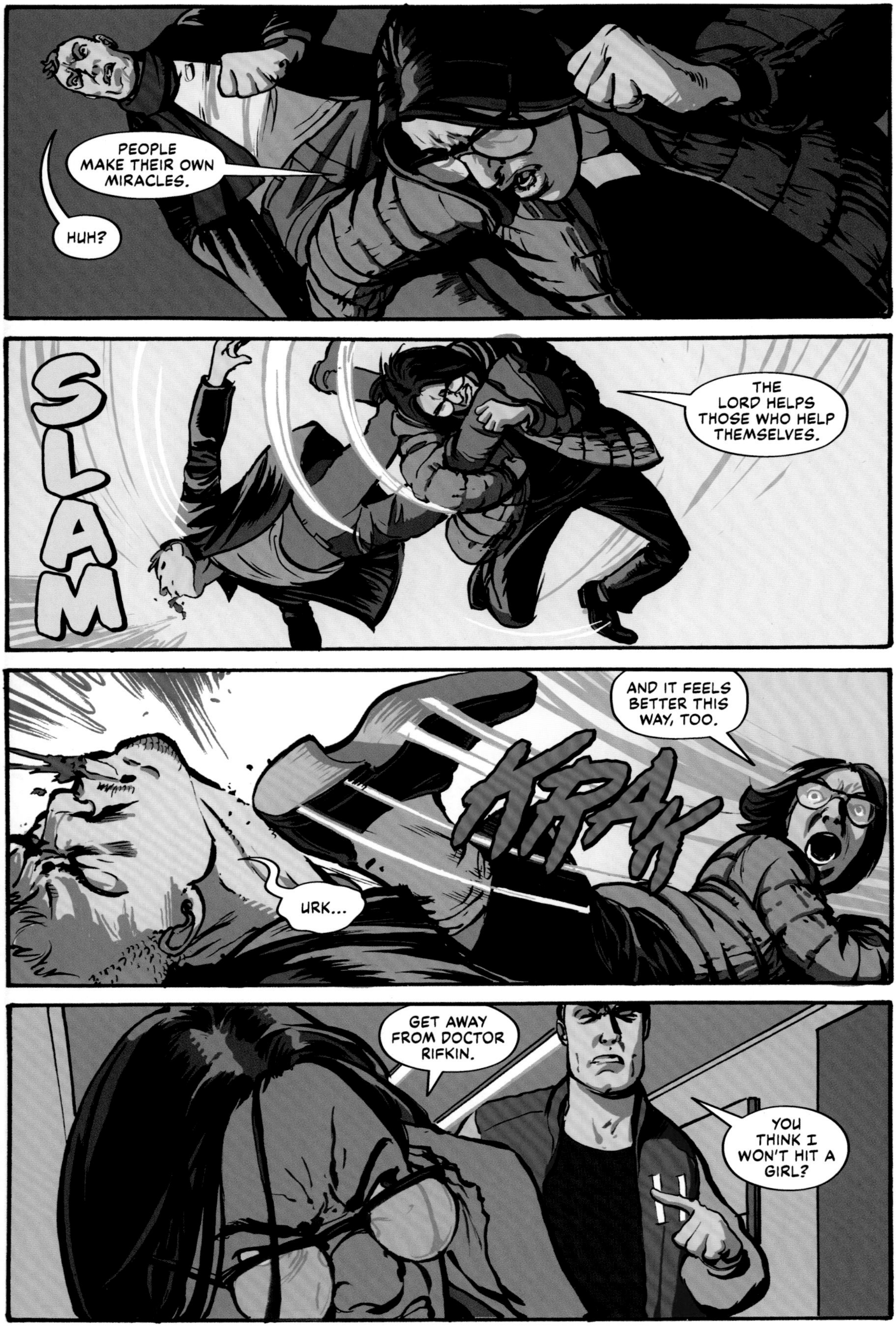
PEOPLE MAKE THEIR OWN MIRACLES.
HUH?
SLAM
THE LORD HELPS THOSE WHO HELP THEMSELVES.
AND IT FEELS BETTER THIS WAY, TOO.
KRAK
URK...
GET AWAY FROM DOCTOR RIFKIN.
YOU THINK I WON'T HIT A GIRL?

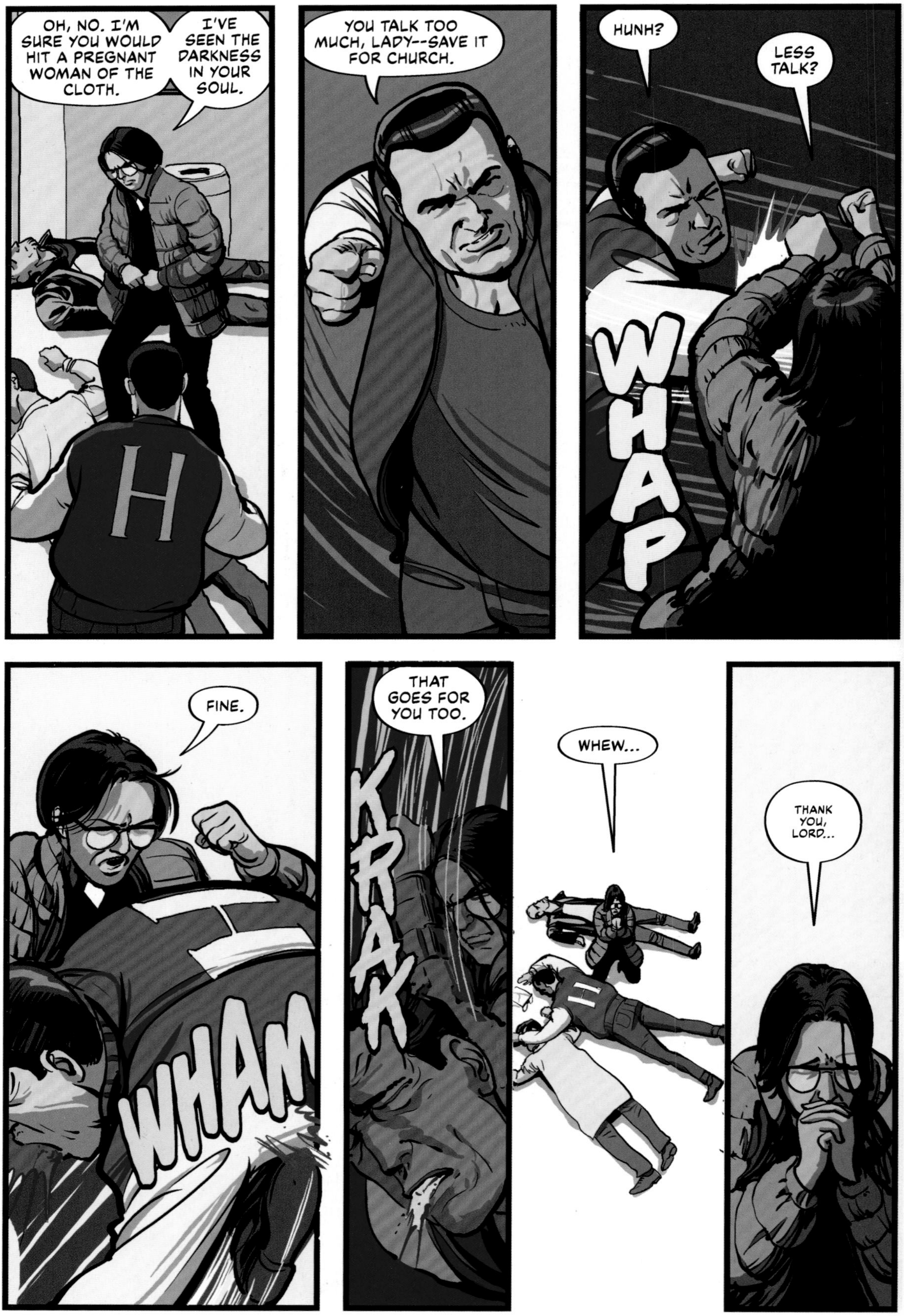
OH, NO. I'M SURE YOU WOULD HIT A PREGNANT WOMAN OF THE CLOTH.
I'VE SEEN THE DARKNESS IN YOUR SOUL.
YOU TALK TOO MUCH, LADY--SAVE IT FOR CHURCH.
HUNH?
LESS TALK?
WHAP
FINE.
WHAM
THAT GOES FOR YOU TOO.
KRAK
WHEW...
THANK YOU, LORD...

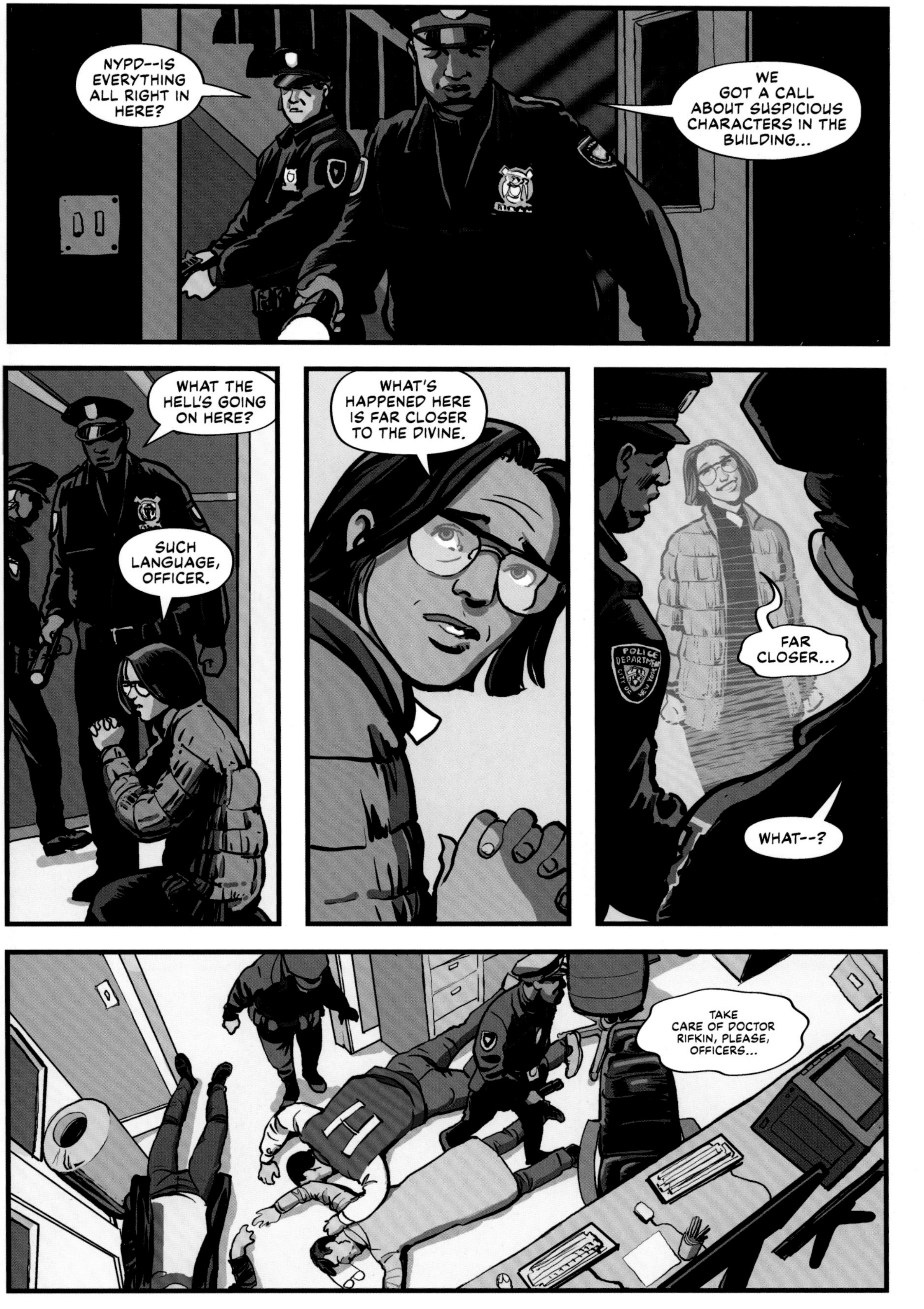
NYPD--IS EVERYTHING ALL RIGHT IN HERE?
WE GOT A CALL ABOUT SUSPICIOUS CHARACTERS IN THE BUILDING...
WHAT THE HELL'S GOING ON HERE?
SUCH LANGUAGE, OFFICER.
WHAT'S HAPPENED HERE IS FAR CLOSER TO THE DIVINE.
FAR CLOSER...
WHAT--?
TAKE CARE OF DOCTOR RIFKIN, PLEASE, OFFICERS...

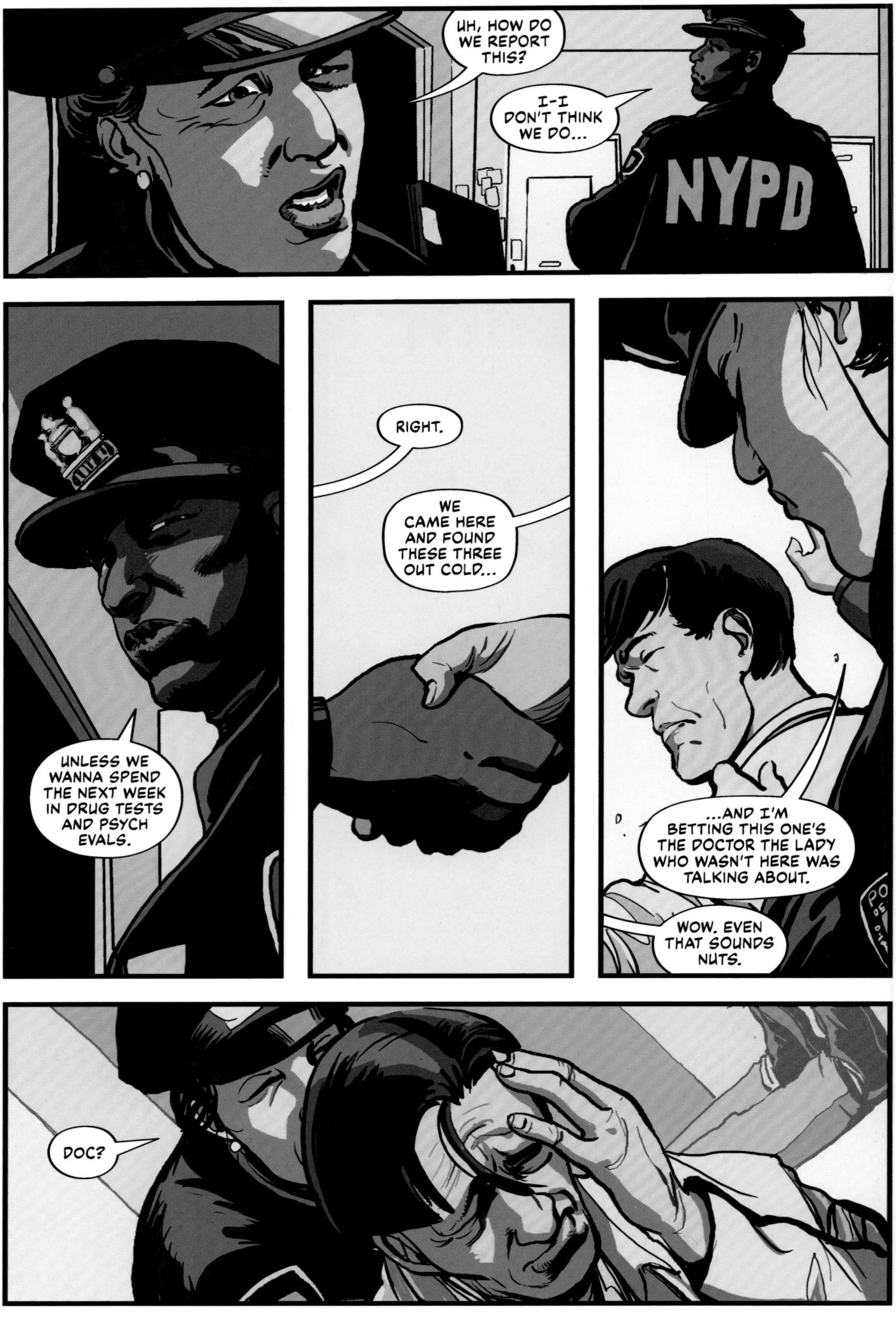
UH, HOW DO WE REPORT THIS?
I-I DON'T THINK WE DO...
NYPD
UNLESS WE WANNA SPEND THE NEXT WEEK IN DRUG TESTS AND PSYCH EVALS.
RIGHT.
WE CAME HERE AND FOUND THESE THREE OUT COLD...
...AND I'M BETTING THIS ONE'S THE DOCTOR THE LADY WHO WASN'T HERE WAS TALKING ABOUT.
WOW. EVEN THAT SOUNDS NUTS.
DOC?

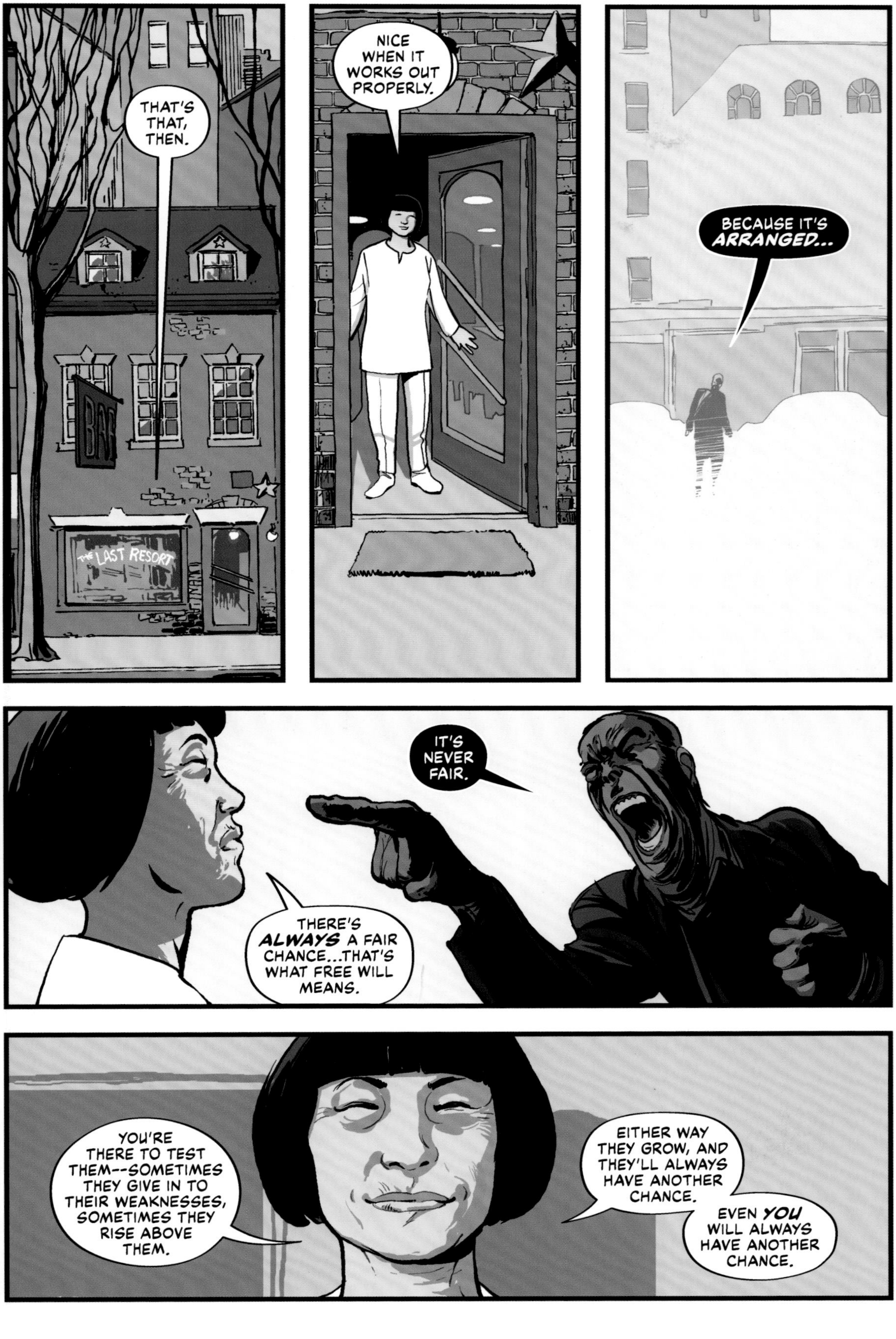
THAT'S THAT, THEN.
NICE WHEN IT WORKS OUT PROPERLY.
BECAUSE IT'S ARRANGED...
IT'S NEVER FAIR.
THERE'S ALWAYS A FAIR CHANCE...THAT'S WHAT FREE WILL MEANS.
THE LAST RESORT
YOU'RE THERE TO TEST THEM--SOMETIMES THEY GIVE IN TO THEIR WEAKNESSES, SOMETIMES THEY RISE ABOVE THEM.
EITHER WAY THEY GROW, AND THEY'LL ALWAYS HAVE ANOTHER CHANCE.
EVEN YOU WILL ALWAYS HAVE ANOTHER CHANCE.

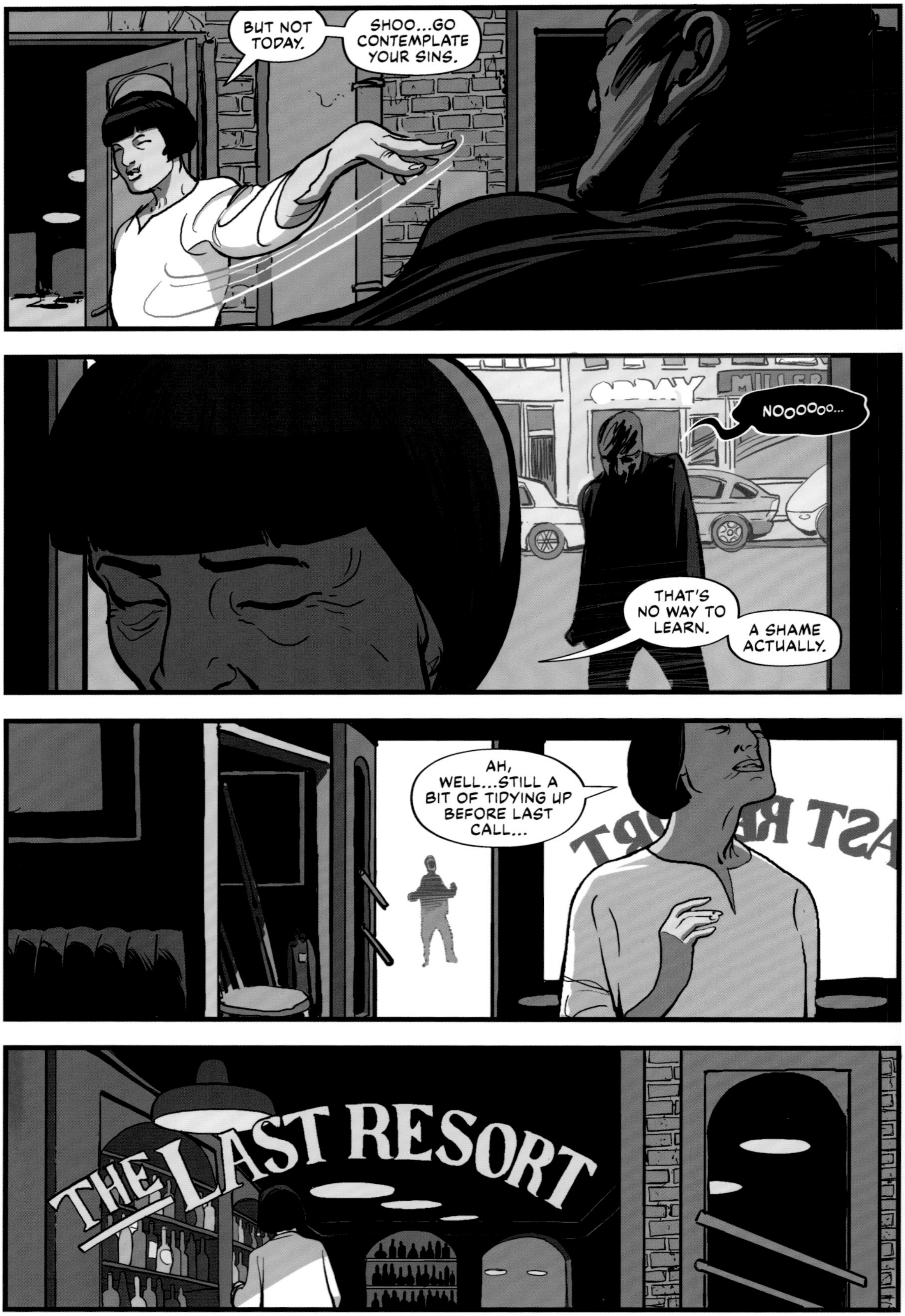
BUT NOT TODAY.
SHOO...GO CONTEMPLATE YOUR SINS.
NOOOOOO...
THAT'S NO WAY TO LEARN.
A SHAME ACTUALLY.
AH, WELL...STILL A BIT OF TIDYING UP BEFORE LAST CALL...
THE LAST RESORT

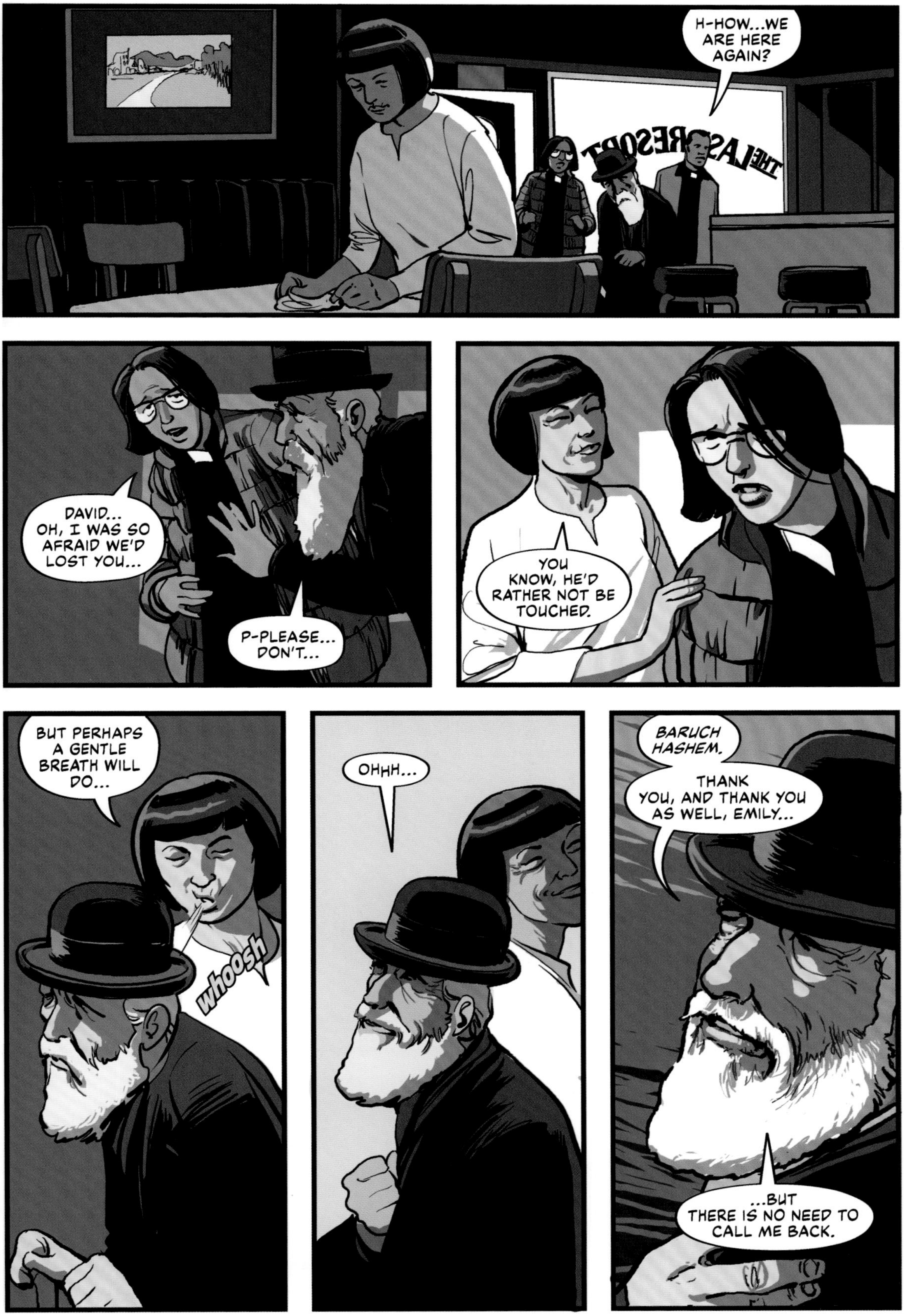
H-HOW...WE ARE HERE AGAIN?
THE LAST RESORT
DAVID... OH, I WAS SO AFRAID WE'D LOST YOU...
P-PLEASE... DON'T...
YOU KNOW, HE'D RATHER NOT BE TOUCHED.
BUT PERHAPS A GENTLE BREATH WILL DO...
whoosh
OHHH...
BARUCH HASHEM.
THANK YOU, AND THANK YOU AS WELL, EMILY...
...BUT THERE IS NO NEED TO CALL ME BACK.

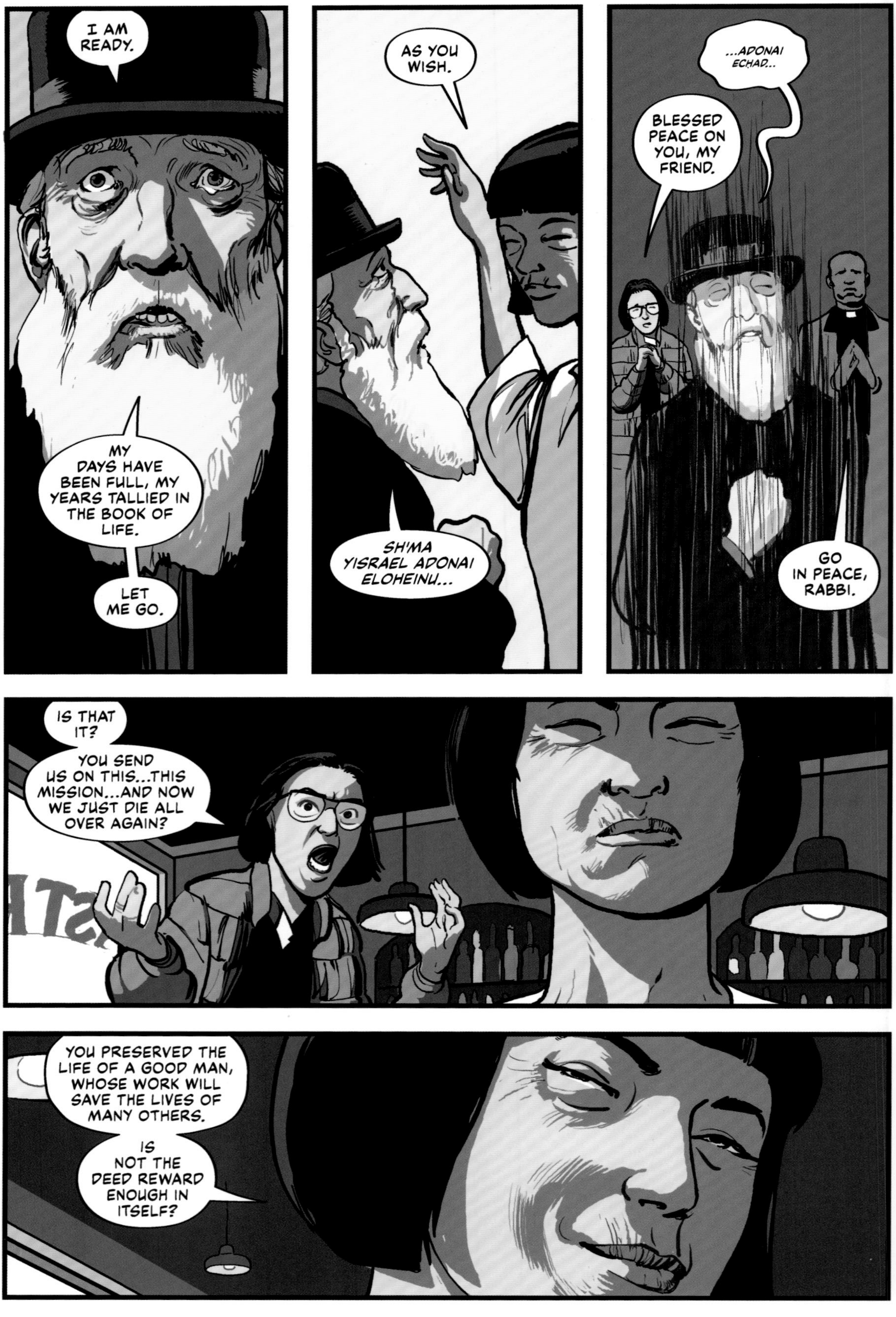
I AM READY.
MY DAYS HAVE BEEN FULL, MY YEARS TALLIED IN THE BOOK OF LIFE.
LET ME GO.
AS YOU WISH.
SH'MA YISRAEL ADONAI ELOHEINU...
...ADONAI ECHAD...
BLESSED PEACE ON YOU, MY FRIEND.
GO IN PEACE, RABBI.
IS THAT IT?
YOU SEND US ON THIS...THIS MISSION...AND NOW WE JUST DIE ALL OVER AGAIN?
YOU PRESERVED THE LIFE OF A GOOD MAN, WHOSE WORK WILL SAVE THE LIVES OF MANY OTHERS.
IS NOT THE DEED REWARD ENOUGH IN ITSELF?

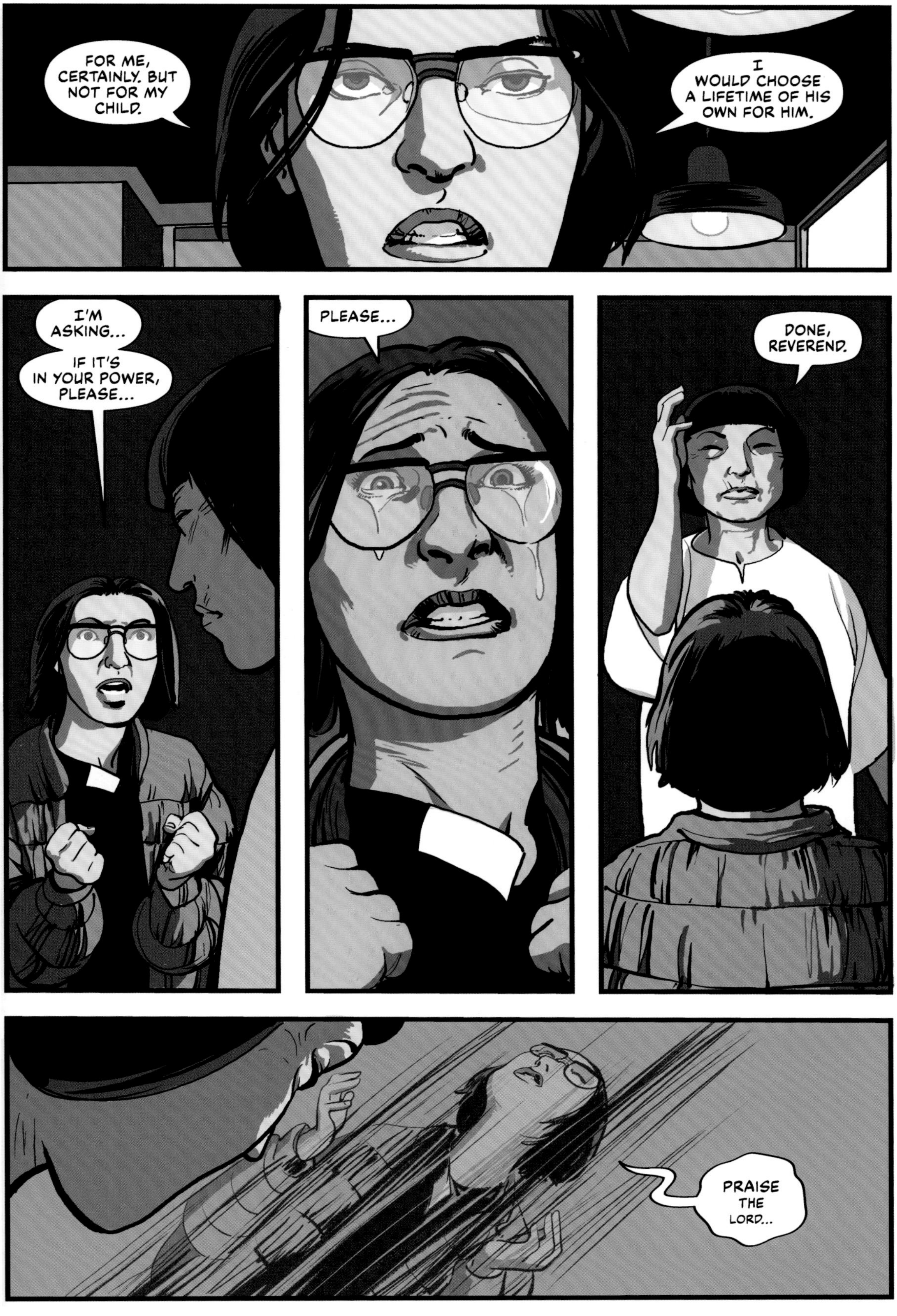
FOR ME, CERTAINLY. BUT NOT FOR MY CHILD.
I WOULD CHOOSE A LIFETIME OF HIS OWN FOR HIM.
I'M ASKING...
IF IT'S IN YOUR POWER, PLEASE...
PLEASE...
DONE, REVEREND.
PRAISE THE LORD...

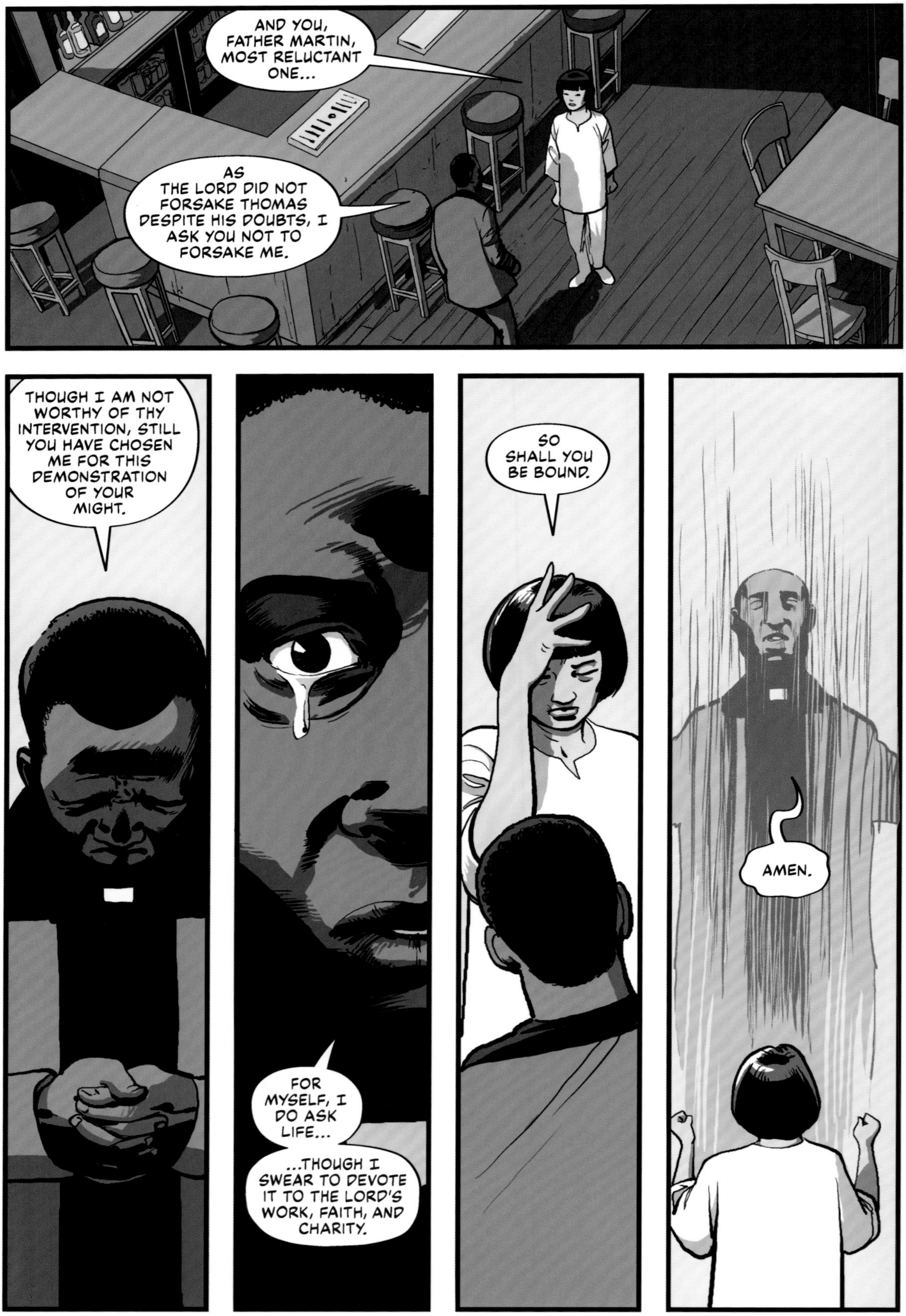
AND YOU, FATHER MARTIN, MOST RELUCTANT ONE...
AS THE LORD DID NOT FORSAKE THOMAS DESPITE HIS DOUBTS, I ASK YOU NOT TO FORSAKE ME.
THOUGH I AM NOT WORTHY OF THY INTERVENTION, STILL YOU HAVE CHOSEN ME FOR THIS DEMONSTRATION OF YOUR MIGHT.
FOR MYSELF, I DO ASK LIFE...
...THOUGH I SWEAR TO DEVOTE IT TO THE LORD'S WORK, FAITH, AND CHARITY.
SO SHALL YOU BE BOUND.
AMEN.

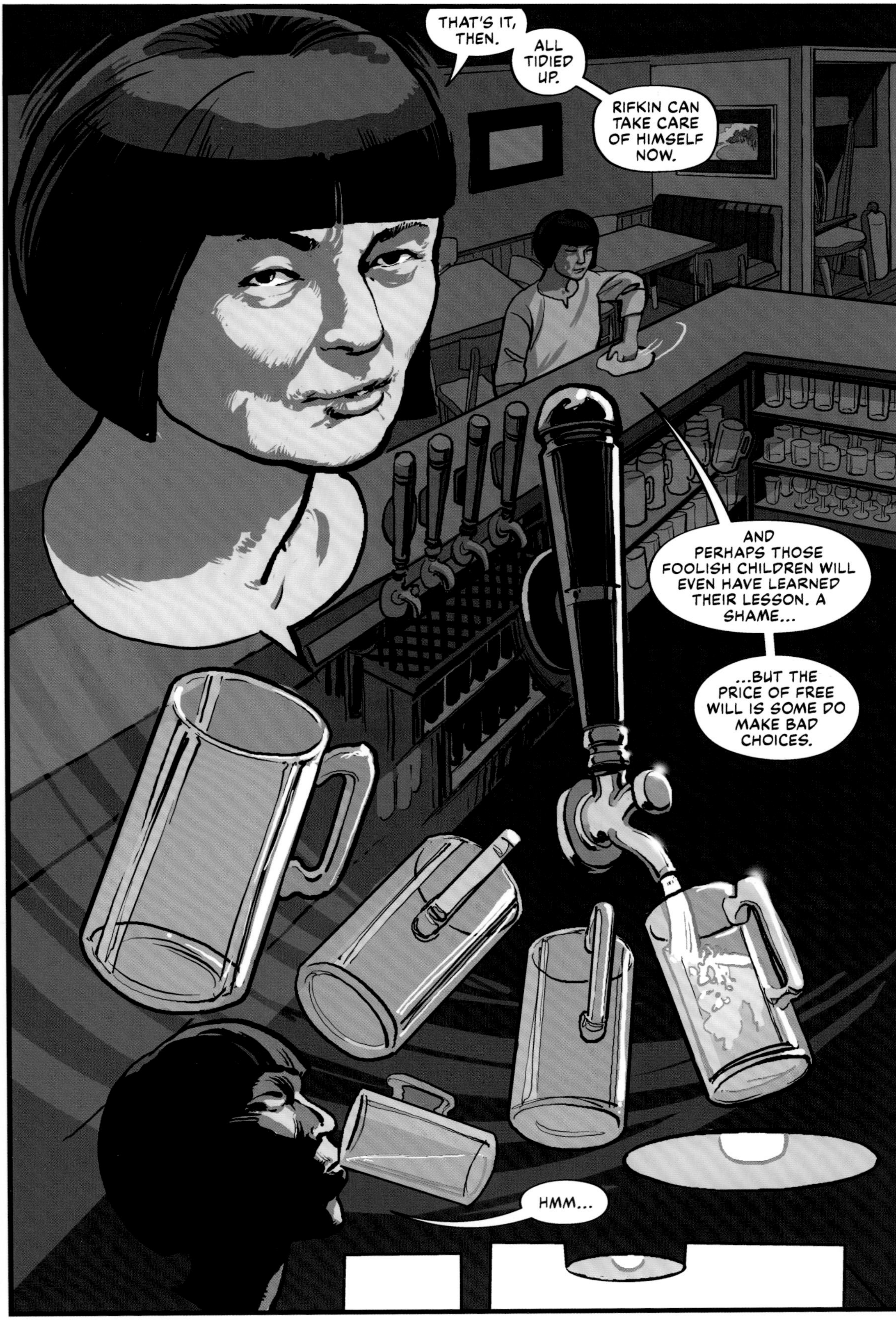
THAT'S IT, THEN.
ALL TIDIED UP.
RIFKIN CAN TAKE CARE OF HIMSELF NOW.
AND PERHAPS THOSE FOOLISH CHILDREN WILL EVEN HAVE LEARNED THEIR LESSON. A SHAME...
...BUT THE PRICE OF FREE WILL IS SOME DO MAKE BAD CHOICES.
HMM...

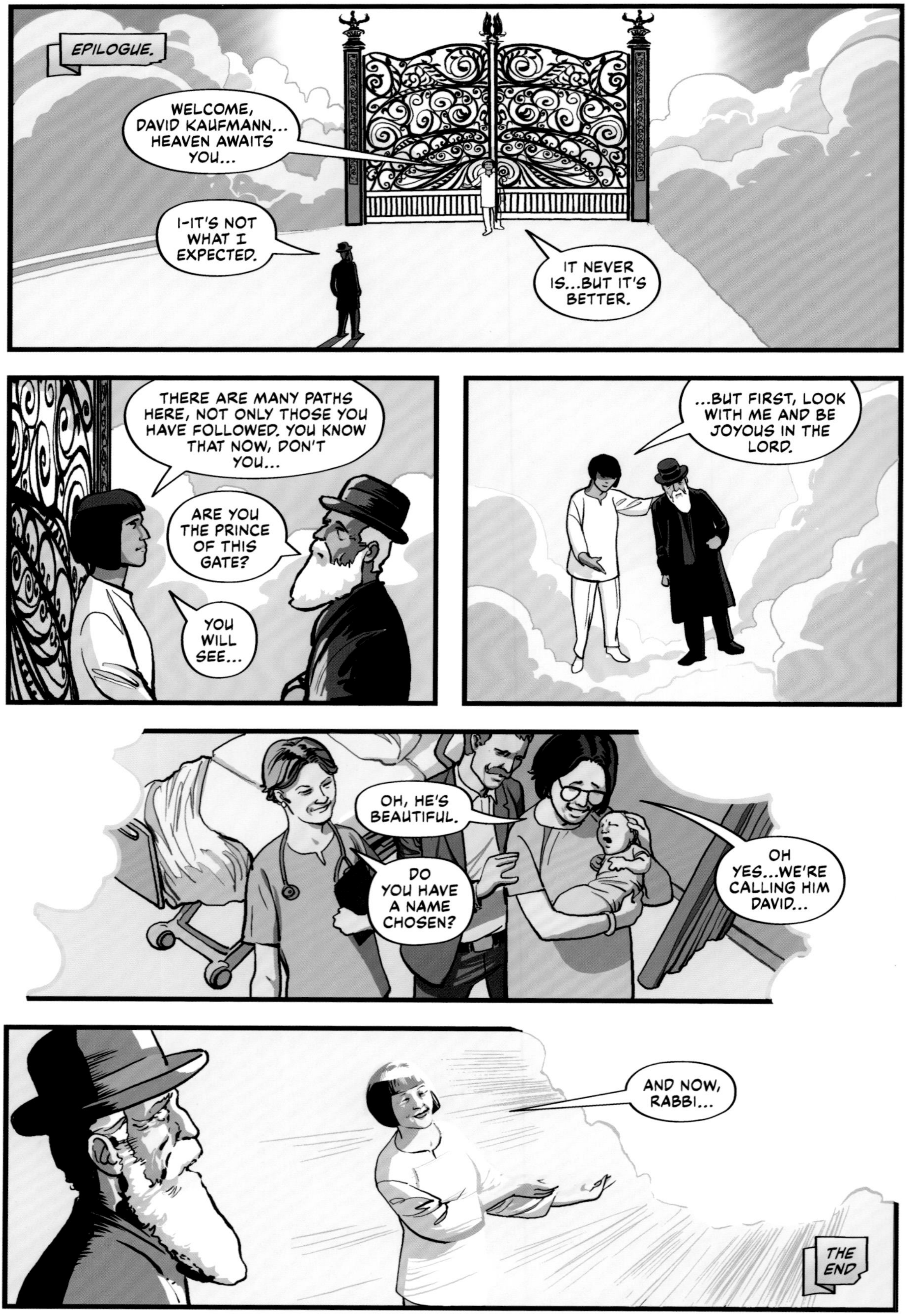
EPILOGUE.
WELCOME, DAVID KAUFMANN... HEAVEN AWAITS YOU...
I-IT'S NOT WHAT I EXPECTED.
IT NEVER IS...BUT IT'S BETTER.
THERE ARE MANY PATHS HERE, NOT ONLY THOSE YOU HAVE FOLLOWED. YOU KNOW THAT NOW, DON'T YOU...
ARE YOU THE PRINCE OF THIS GATE?
YOU WILL SEE...
...BUT FIRST, LOOK WITH ME AND BE JOYOUS IN THE LORD.
OH, HE'S BEAUTIFUL.
DO YOU HAVE A NAME CHOSEN?
OH YES...WE'RE CALLING HIM DAVID...
AND NOW, RABBI...
THE END

AFTERWORD

Confession: I am not a religious man. While I was born into a long line of the Jewish faith and tradition, I never adopted the complexities of organized religion as a personal faith. In fact, my bar mitzvah consisted of phonetically reciting the blessings over the Torah (instead of reciting the lengthy Torah portion as is usually required), so anxious were the teachers to get rid of a difficult student.

That said, I have great respect for those of genuine faith in a higher power, both members of my own family (Jewish and Catholic) and friends (of many traditions). Ours is a stunningly complex and beautiful world, and we understand only a fraction of it. In my lifetime, I've seen a constant and rapid progression of knowledge revealing its mysteries, a journey that seems far from over. (Gut flora can affect mental attitudes?) If faith helps you navigate this life, more power to it.

In writing this graphic novel, then, I am indebted to those wiser in the ways of formal religion than I. In particular, my friends the Reverend Canon Chuck Robertson, Ph. D. and Rabbi Matt Futterman, both of whom I thank for their patience. And this book would not exist without my dear departed friend, Rabbi Dr. David Kaufmann, whose long conversations with me I hope this volume honors. None of them are responsible for any errors or omissions or heresies herein, which are all my own.

--Paul Levitz

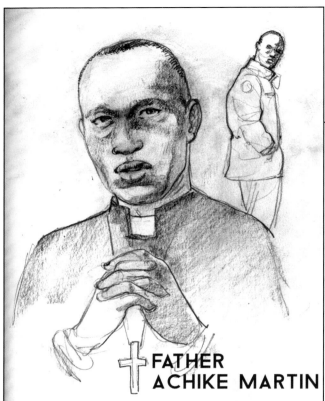

FATHER
ACHIKE MARTIN

GALLERY
Notes by Simon Fraser.

REVEREND
EMILY MOORE

FATHER ACHIKE MARTIN. A priest from Nigeria. I based him on my friend Julius Mapambano Jackson, who was actually Tanzanian. East and West Africans do actually look quite different, but I traded authenticity for familiarity in this case. Julius was my first gym trainer and was crowned Mr. Arusha at least once. He sadly died 13 years ago of HIV/AIDS related illness aged 25 years old, so I've aged him up to around 38, which he would have been if he was still with us.

EMILY MOORE. I based her on another friend of mine, Jessica Bathhurst, an actor and educator here in New York. It's not a good likeness of Jess at all, but I like her determination and confidence and I wanted Emily to have that. I hear the voice of Jess when I draw Emily.

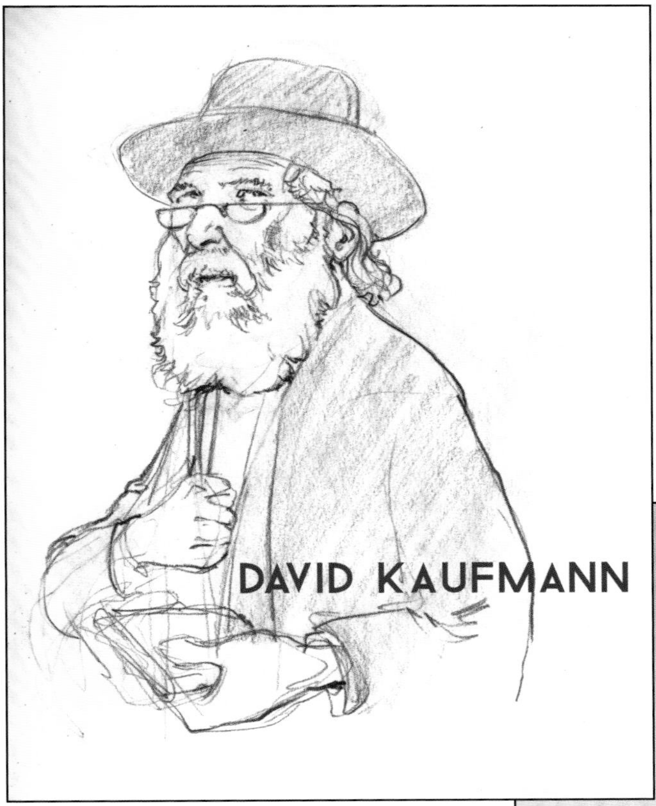
DAVID KAUFMANN

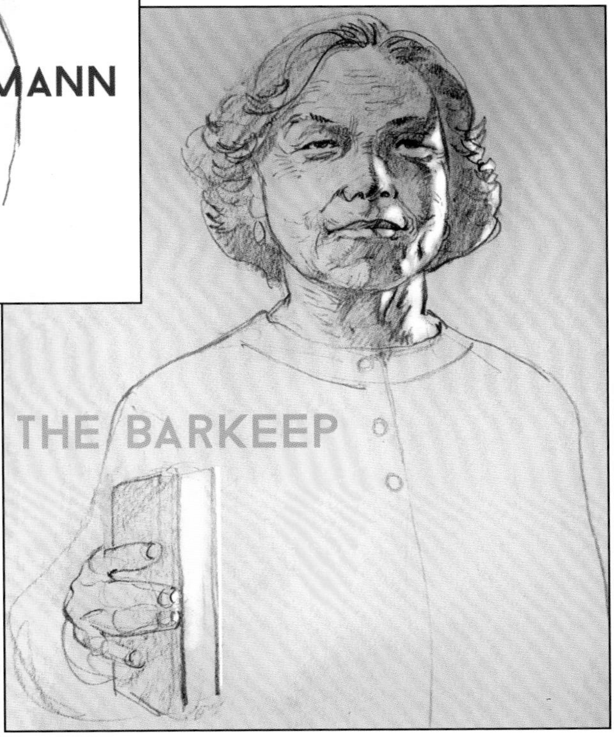
THE BARKEEP

RABBI DAVID KAUFMAN. I actually saw this guy on the 1 train here in Manhattan. There are several orthodox Jewish enclaves here in New York, including where I lived in Crown Heights, Brooklyn. I surreptitiously watched this fellow out of the corner of my eye, then drew him from memory as soon as I got some paper and a pencil. I would have never invented a Rabbi character who looked so stereotypical, but this guy was such perfect casting for Kaufman that I couldn't resist.

THE BARKEEP. The initial script implied a more traditional Irish barman type, but I wanted to sidestep expectations here. If this character is an aspect of the Almighty then I liked that she be a woman, not white, and difficult to judge exactly how old she is. Her apparent age seems to vary during the story, which I'm calling a feature, not a bug.

PAUL LEVITZ is a comics industry legend, with a career spanning over forty years as a writer, editor, and publishing executive. Raised in Brooklyn, New York, Paul began making waves in the comics world as a teenager, editing *The Comic Reader*, the first regularly published comics news fanzine. Paul began to accept freelance work for DC Comics, writing text and letter pages, which led to an editorial position at DC in 1973. Paul moved from editor to vice president to executive vice president and served as president and publisher from 2002 to 2009. Paul's writing résumé includes *Wonder Woman*, *Batman*, *Doctor Fate*, and countless other titles, including his memorable run as the writer of *The Legion of Super-Heroes*, over 150 issues written between 1977 and 2013. In 2010, Paul's *75 Years of DC Comics: The Art of Modern Mythmaking* saw publication, winning the 2011 Will Eisner Comic Industry Award for Best Comics-Related Book. Paul was enshrined in the Eisner Hall of Fame in 2019. Since leaving DC Comics in 2009, Paul has taught at Columbia University, Pace University, and Manhattanville College and currently sits on the boards of the Comic Book Legal Defense Fund, the Clarion Foundation, and Boom! Studios while still adding to his long list of writing credits. To follow Paul, go to paullevitz.com and facebook.com/paul.levitz.

SIMON FRASER is originally from Scotland and now resides in Brooklyn, New York. Simon first came to the attention of comics readers with his collaboration with novelist Martin Millar on *Lux & Alby Sign On and Save the Universe* in 1992. This led to work in *Tiger* and *Judge Dredd* magazines, and then to the co-creation with writer Robbie Morrison of *Nikolai Dante*, debuting in 1997 in *2000 AD* magazine. Simon has gone on to a number of projects, including *Family* in *Judge Dredd*, *Richard Matheson's Hell House* for IDW, and the project for which he is best known Stateside, Mark Millar's *Kingsman: The Red Diamond*, collected in 2018. Follow Simon on Twitter: twitter.com/simonfraser

GARY CALDWELL from Aberdeen, Scotland is a longtime illustrator and colorist, best known for his work in countless issues of *2000 AD* (including *Nikolai Dante* with Simon Fraser) as well as *Judge Dredd*, *Doctor Who*, and many more.

NATE PIEKOS founded Blambot in 1999 and has created some of the comic industry's most popular fonts and has lettered stories for every major American comics publisher. Nate's work has also been featured in product packaging, video games, on television, and in feature film. His software has been licensed by Microsoft, Six Flags, *The New Yorker*, The Gap, and many other corporate clients. Nate's fonts and other interesting lettering info are available at his website, blambot.com, and his ongoing webcomic, *Atland*, can be found at realmofatland.com.